The Street-Smart Side of Business

The Street-Smart Side of Business

A Behind-the-Scenes Guide to Inspire Forward Thinking

Tara Acosta

BUSINESS EXPERT PRESS

Leader in applied, concise business books

The Street-Smart Side of Business:
A Behind-the-Scenes Guide to Inspire Forward Thinking

First published in 2021 by
Business Expert Press, LLC
222 East 46th Street, New York, NY 10017
www.businessexpertpress.com

ISBN-13: 978-1-63742-131-4 (paperback)
ISBN-13: 978-1-63742-132-1 (e-book)

Business Expert Press Business Career Development Collection

Collection ISSN: 2642-2123 (print)
Collection ISSN: 2642-2131 (electronic)

First edition: 2021

10 9 8 7 6 5 4 3 2 1

This book is dedicated to my husband who is an excellent representation of all the positive, optimistic, and extremely hard working entrepreneurs out there.

Description

This book is for all the spirited entrepreneurs out there who want to learn about the inner workings of starting up or investing in an established business. Get ready to peek behind the curtain and see what really happens from behind the scenes. Within these pages, you will read about stories of business successes and business failures. I hope to teach you what to look for and think about before entering any business venture.

For any business, the fundamental goal is to be different and to be better than those with whom you are competing. So as you read, get ready to absorb some of the most useful information you will ever hear. It's not really available anywhere else.

The content of this book is designed to motivate and prepare those who have an interest in being a business owner and to give them realistic insight so that they can be prepared for all aspects of business. It explains through examples of why it is critical to make informed and educated decisions and to go beyond the obvious, and to be in tune with the motives and emotions of all parties involved. When poor decisions are made, there are explanations given of what led to the emerging problems: poor information, poor analysis, a lack of asking the right questions to those individuals under consideration. The point is to understand exactly what you're getting into and not be blinded by the appearance of a good opportunity.

This book was written during the COVID-19 pandemic, which was one of the most uncertain times in our world's history. Some businesses were devastated and some businesses thrived. I am sending you all positive energy and encouraging you to find the courage to open yourself up and step out of your comfort zone and get down to business. After reading *The Street-Smart Side of Business* you will have all the tools you need in your business arsenal.

Keywords

entrepreneurs; ethics; integrity; ownership; attitudes; career success; organization; customer service; promotion; business plan; leadership; loyalty; managing; personal experience

Contents

Introduction

When I started out as a small business owner, I wish someone had prepared me for certain possibilities. I hope to teach you what to look for and think about before entering any business venture.

You know the old phrase, "Every lesson learned is the hard lesson learned." There is so much truth to that, but if we open ourselves up to listening, really listening and absorbing information presented to us, it doesn't have to be. You just have to use your smarts. Your book smarts are important, but your street-smarts are necessary. So, as you read on, get ready to absorb some of the most useful information you will ever hear, and put it to use.

Many established business owners have journeyed through the successes and the hardships of running a business. It is unfortunate that most of them have to learn the hard way that in both solo-run businesses and in partnerships, not everything goes according to plan. All parties involved may start out on the same page, but it is not often that everyone stays there. It takes work and constant communication in order to avoid unnecessary drama. When going into business you are taking a chance. There is always risk involved. The grit and grind that is needed for success, isn't for just anyone. And even for those that have an extremely strong work ethic, stuff happens and things can go wrong. So, it is important to prepare for the worst while working toward the best.

This book is meant to clue you in on what to look for in a potentially successful business opportunity. More importantly, it focuses on what red flags you should not ignore. Through examples and short stories, you are going to learn how to use your intuition, listen to your gut feelings, and utilize your street-smarts.

Businesses do not run themselves; people run a business. Make sure you understand how to know exactly who you're dealing with before going into business with them.

COVID-19 shook our world as we knew it. The examples cited in *The Street-Smart Side of Business* were written before the pandemic but their messages are timeless and will be as applicable in the future as when they took place. This may be the time to start giving serious thought about the career possibility you always wondered about: to have your own business. It is the creative space that has been living inside you. Now may well be the time to analyze the options that will best serve you and your talents going forward. It is never too late for something new, if you want it to happen.

So before you take a leap of faith and start that business, make sure you prepare yourself and read this book thoroughly to get an understanding of what's on the other side of a business venture. Trust me, you want to know about business from the surface and from behind the scenes. It's not meant to scare you, it's meant to bring awareness.

I can't talk to each of you in person, so consider this book as your stand-in mentor to help you achieve important personal and business goals.

—Tara Acosta

CHAPTER 1

Pick Your Poison

Figure 1 *What do you want to be when you grow up?*

Photo: Fergregory/iStock by Getty Images

"What do you want to be when you grow up?" We all know that to be an infamous question at all ages and stages of life. Many adults are still trying to figure it out.

There are a small percentage of people who know the answer to that question early on. Teachers, police officers, and medical providers may possibly be a few. A survey says that most people in these professions have wanted to do what they are doing from early on. For those of us who don't know exactly what we want to be, we have a harder time trying to figure that out. Most people have no idea what their career path is going to be when they enter into college.

Our society as a whole has set up something that I can't quite wrap my mind around. We have a very important decision to make and at a very young age. It's crazy to me that we expect kids to make one of the potentially largest financial investments of their life at 17 or 18 years old, with literally no experience in what they are about to invest in.

This is where our education system is severely lacking. There is not enough exposure for our students to get a realistic understanding of what different careers actually entail. I would love to see more career days or career weeks built into our educational agenda. To allow a student to see the day-to-day grind behind different professions would be incredibly helpful. Unfortunately, in current times most kids go in blind.

Deciding their college career path is an incredibly important and expensive decision. During the next four years (at least), they will spend time, energy, and lots of money studying. In their studies, college students will learn about a lot of different things around a specific career path as well as a broad spectrum of classes and topics that they may never need. But being educated is always a positive in a person's life. Hopefully, what they are reading and learning can really prepare them for that career. A college education is a good source of basic information. The most important part of a college is the fact that a degree is necessary to be hired in today's corporate world, but let's face it, the real learning comes from-the-job training and experiences.

College is a business. Our society has made it so that this business structure is a necessary part of financial success, for most people. Yet it is a huge financial setback if Mommy and Daddy weren't able to properly save for little Johnny's or little Mary's college education. As the saying goes, "Ya gotta have money to make money," if you don't be prepared to be paying those loans off for a long time. Unless you were given the gift of being book smarts or athletic, in which you may be able to get that free educational ride. I mean free as in money, you pay for it in many other ways. In these cases, a student sacrifices to work hard at their studies and/or activities.

If you don't go to college and end up getting into a trade, then good for you. There's good money to be made in the trades. Not to mention you gain a solid skill set. But be prepared for the judgment. Unfortunately, in the company of a certain type of crowd there may be judgment for not having that trusty, expensive diploma.

C'mon, don't act like you don't know what I mean. Let's say you're at a dinner party with your new girlfriend or boyfriend and their family. The education topic comes up and everyone proudly announces what they have their degrees in and what elite colleges they attended. Here you have Joey at the end of the table. He says that he didn't go to college and he's a plumber. There's a silent but noticeable thing that happens. What, you wonder? You know what. It's just lingering in the air, that thing without a name. You know it's true. Then someone politely tries to defend the trades. They say things like "You can make good money being a plumber," or "My neighbor's cousin is a plumber and he always has a wad of cash in his pocket," or "College isn't for everyone." All these statements are true, but in this crowd of people who have multiple degrees, you better believe there is judgment happening. But don't worry, Mr. Plumber, because chances are you are just as successful as they are, minus the degree.

When kids/young adults don't know exactly which direction they want to go in life, they start off undecided in their studies. Then a lot of these kids/young adults go with the business major route. With a degree in business you cover a plethora of things. You can take that degree and apply it to almost any field. But is it really necessary? Education will always broaden your career options and that is a fact. The work that you put in will enhance your life. But the truth is that you do not need a diploma to open a business. What you need is money, resources, and ambition, and of course the proper licenses.

Think about what makes you happy. Consider that whatever you do in life you will be spending a considerable amount of time doing it. If you love what you do, it's doesn't feel like work. It feels like you're being paid to do what you love. That is priceless. What makes it priceless is the fact that most people do not know how to turn their passion into income. So, for those of us who are able to figure that out, consider yourself lucky. This is the best part about being an entrepreneur. Being able to take your passion and turn it into your livelihood.

Now the last thing that I want to do is talk anyone out of college. Education at a college level is a beautiful thing. Education at any level is a beautiful thing. The world that we live in today requires education. It requires a degree or multiple degrees. But here's a secret: in all reality all the degrees in the world can't prepare you for the ugly side of business.

This is what brought me to writing *The Street-Smart Side of Business*. This is the part that no college course can prepare you for, so get ready. I want you to learn how to take a sip before you drink the whole bottle.

Questions

1. What do you want to be when finishing your education and why are you attracted to this profession or business?

   _____

   _____

   _____

2. What steps are you going to take to get there?

   _____

   _____

   _____

3. What do you think about our education or training system?

   _____

   _____

   _____

4. Do you believe that our education system prepares you for the real world?

   _____

   _____

   _____

5. Why? Why not?

   _____

   _____

   _____

6. What changes would you make in the education system?

   _____

   _____

   _____

Journal

What did you take from this chapter?

_____

_____

_____

_____

_____

CHAPTER 2

Burst Your Bubble

Figure 2 Being a business owner isn't always rainbows and sunshine

Photo: Julianna funk/iStock by Getty Images

You decide to start your own business. You have come across an opportunity of a lifetime doing what you love, and you're going for it! Owning a business of any size is a huge responsibility. It takes a lot of time, energy, and work. It takes grit. It's like becoming a parent for the first time. And this applies to every new business that you take on. You have to love it, nurture it, and understand that it's going to have a significant impact on your life, both immediately and long term. You're going to have long days and sleepless nights. **Your goal will be planning on how to raise the best business that you can possibly raise**.

Let's start out with the business plan. Anyone can make anything sound good. All it takes is a good sales pitch. People can even make a business look good on paper. But the importance of a business plan is necessary! If you're going to spend the time creating a business concept and selling it to investors, make sure you spend the time developing a proper business plan. See Chapter 3 for detailed information on how to write a business plan.

A general business plan outline is the basic format of what you will need to research and plan before you get your business up and running. Not only does it help you set your goals in a realistic manner but it also prepares you for most aspects of running a business. It will give insight on things that you may have not given thought to. If you do your proper due diligence, you will see that the only thing that a business plan is really missing is how to evaluate those that you may need to deal with. It doesn't provide guidance on how to be a good judge of character and try to protect yourself from potential scam artists. Sadly, they are out there and more than you'd like to think. They come in all shapes and sizes and lots of disguises. But that's why you're reading this book. You're going to finish this book loaded with useful information that you would never have given a thought to. Why wouldn't you think about the information in this book? Well, most likely because you're a good person who wants to learn how to be a smart and savvy businessperson.

You are a motivated entrepreneur who is in a positive mindset. You have successful goals and planning on doing great things. This book will put you in tune with how to avoid a negative business path. Exhausted yet? No, good! You're going to need a lot of energy to gather all of this information correctly and efficiently for your new business. But at least you will now have some basic guidelines to go from. And just so you know there are professionals out there that help work through your business plan. So don't skip this step, or your business bubble just may end up bursting.

Let's say that there is a couple who each own their own business. Even though they are married, they run their business separately. They also run their business very differently.

She is a professional and a scholar with multiple degrees. She had a stable upbringing in a nurturing environment.

He has a high school diploma and a career in the service industry. His upbringing was far from stable and he had much adversity to overcome.

She owns and operates her businesses with more of a hands-on approach and wears many hats. He has a few business ventures as well.

He runs his business from behind the scenes and is better at delegating roles to different people whom he employs. Nonetheless, they are both successful entrepreneurs. They both can learn from each other.

Why the back story? For starters, it's pretty much the point of this book. You see, when someone is raised in a near "perfect" setting they don't realize that sometimes in life people can be outright dirty. When children are raised in a safety bubble they only see the world in a positive light. They see the world through innocent eyes. It is an upbringing in which most parents want to raise their children. Keeping them sheltered from all the bad things in the world is the goal of so many parents. These kids usually grow up to be very kind, trusting, extremely optimistic, and unfortunately sometimes very naive adults.

When someone is raised in a street-style setting, there is early insight as to what the world is made of, the good, the bad and everything in between. Kids are exposed to how crazy the world can be. Exposure to real-life situations of bad things that happen isn't the worst thing. Now I'm not suggesting you throw your kid out of the house to go live on the streets, but I am suggesting that you have real talks with them. Don't cover up every little thing, let them know that some people can make really bad decisions. Let them out of that bubble.

Now there's the flip side. What does being from a "bubble" upbringing have to offer? Well for starters, support. If you are from a home with two parents in a nurturing household, chances are you're ahead of the game. You have two people who are working together to provide you with the best opportunities. They want what's best for you and are working and making sacrifices to be able to provide you with that. If you're going to a private school, there is a heavy expense that is being paid. And I have a secret for anyone who thinks that kids in a private school are privileged, they are. But I have news for you, the tuition fairy doesn't exist. There are people that grinding hard and working their butts off to provide their kids with a good education. Even the kids who are on scholarships, there is no scholarship fairy either. Hardworking people donate their hard-earned money to help out someone who may not be in the financial position to have this opportunity. So, no matter how you look at it, it is expensive to be alive. And it takes grit and perseverance to create a nice life for yourself and your family.

Always remember that sometimes even with the best work ethic and the best of intentions, sometimes life throws you a curveball. So, grind while you have the opportunity to because it may not always be an option. What do I mean? Something as basic as your health, it's the thing we take for granted the most. It can be taken away in a blink.

This isn't a parenting book. It's a book that is going to shed light on what can go wrong and how to try to avoid negative things from happening. It's a reminder that you have to be a good parent to your business. It's a book about the potentially ugly side of business. For those of you who are experienced business owners, you may know where I'm going with this. For those of you who are new to the game or are thinking about getting into business, you may be a little taken back by the verbiage I use as I go on. Sorry, not sorry, but this is business.

Questions

1. Why do you think a business owner would want to wear many hats and take on many roles?

   _____

   _____

   _____

2. Why do you think a business owner would want to delegate different roles to different people?

   _____

   _____

   _____

3. Do you think you would want to be involved in all aspects in your business? Why? Why not?

   _____

   _____

   _____

4. Would you want to have a business partner? Why? Why not?

   _____

   _____

   _____

Journal

What did you take from this chapter?

_____

_____

_____

_____

_____

CHAPTER 3

What's the Plan, Stan?

Figure 3 Business planning

Photo: Fizkes/iStock by Getty Images

As I mentioned, there are a lot of sources to assist in composing a business plan. You can do a general online search and have an overload of options. That can be both a blessing and a curse. Sometimes too many options can be very overwhelming. Reviews are helpful, but always keep in mind that scorned people are more likely to take the time to write negative reviews. One of the best sources for information is the U.S. Small Business Administration. Again, it can be a bit of information overload, but you would rather have too much than not enough. If you are feeling overwhelmed, you can also seek guidance from your local community business associations. Your local associations can be an excellent source of hands-on guidance. They can help connect you with people in their local network to work side by side with you. It is comforting to know that a professional is coming recommended by people in your own community. Referrals are always the best type of advertising, and the most trusted.

Listed below is information sourced from the U.S. Small Business Administration. It is a good general breakdown of the steps you will want to take.

Plan Your Business

Write Your Business Plan

Source: U.S. Small Business Administration

- Calculate your start-up costs.
- Fund your business.
- Buy an existing business or franchise.

Your business plan is the foundation of your business. Learn how to write a business plan quickly and efficiently with a business plan template.

Business Plans Help You Run Your Business

A good business plan guides you through each stage of starting and managing your business. You'll use your business plan as a roadmap for how to structure, run, and grow your new business. It's a way to think through the key elements of your business.

Business plans can help you get funding or bring on new business partners. Investors want to feel confident that they'll see a return on their investment. Your business plan is the tool you'll use to convince people that working with you—or investing in your company—is a smart choice.

Pick a Business Plan Format That Works for You

There's no right or wrong way to write a business plan. What's important is that your plan meets your needs.

Most business plans fall into one of two common categories: traditional or lean start-up.

Traditional business plans are more common, use a standard structure, and encourage you to go into detail in each section. They tend to require more work upfront and can be dozens of pages long.

Lean start-up business plans are less common but still use a standard structure. They focus on summarizing only the most important points of the key elements of your plan. They can take as little as one hour to make and are typically only one page.

Whether you choose to write a lean business plan or a traditional business plan, they both will contain the same basic information.

Executive Summary

- Briefly tell your reader what your company is and why it will be successful.
- Include your mission statement, your product or service, and basic information about your company's leadership team, employees, and location.
- You should also include financial information and high-level growth plans if you plan to ask for financing.

Company Description

Use your company description to provide detailed information about your company. Your company description is the place to boast about your strengths.

- Go into detail about the problems your business solves. Be specific, and list out the consumers, organization, or businesses your company plans to serve.
- Explain the competitive advantages that will make your business a success.
- Are there experts on your team?
- Have you found the perfect location for your store?

Market Analysis

You'll need a good understanding of your industry outlook and target market. Competitive research will show you what other businesses are doing and what their strengths are. In your market research, look for trends and themes.

- What do successful competitors do?
- Why does it work?
- Can you do it better?

Now's the time to answer these questions.

Organization and Management

Tell your reader how your company will be structured and who will run it.

- Describe the legal structure of your business. State whether you have or intend to incorporate your business as a C or an S corporation;
- Form a general or limited partnership; or
- If you're a sole proprietor or Limited Liability Company (LLC).

Use an organizational chart to lay out who's in charge of what in your company. Show how each person's unique experience will contribute to the success of your venture. Consider including resumes and CVs of key members of your team.

Service or Product Line

Describe what you sell or what service you offer.

- Explain how it benefits your customers and what the product lifecycle looks like.
- Share your plans for intellectual property, like copyright or patent filings.

- If you're doing research and development for your service or product, explain it in detail.

Marketing and Sales

Your approach to a marketing strategy should reflect your understanding of your market. It is a living document that should evolve and change to fit your unique needs and possible shifts in your market.

Your goal in this section is to describe how you'll attract and retain customers or clients. You'll also describe how a sale will actually happen. You'll refer to this section later when you make financial projections, so make sure to thoroughly describe your complete marketing and sales strategies.

Funding Request

If you're asking for funding, this is where you'll outline your funding requirements. Your goal is to clearly explain how much funding you'll need over the next five years and what you'll use it for.

- Specify whether you want debt or equity, the terms you'd like applied, and the length of time your request will cover.
- Give a detailed description of how you'll use your funds.
- Specify if you need funds to buy equipment or materials, pay salaries, or cover specific bills until revenue increases.
- Always include a description of your future strategic financial plans, like paying off debt or selling your business.

Financial Projections

Supplement your funding request with financial projections. Your goal is to convince the reader that your business is stable and will be a financial success.

- If your business is already established, include income statements, balance sheets, and cash flow statements for the last three to five years.

- If you have other collateral you could put against a loan, make sure to list it now.
- Provide a prospective financial outlook for the next five years. Include forecasted income statements, balance sheets, cash flow statements, and capital expenditure budgets. For the first year, be even more specific and use quarterly—or even monthly—projections.
- Make sure to clearly explain your projections, and match them to your funding requests.

This is a great place to use graphs and charts to tell the financial story of your business.

Lean Start-Up Plan

You might prefer a lean start-up format if you want to explain or start your business quickly, your business is relatively simple, or you plan to regularly change and refine your business plan.

Lean start-up formats are charts that use only a handful of elements to describe your company's value proposition, infrastructure, customers, and finances. They're useful for visualizing trade-offs and fundamental facts about your company.

There are many versions of lean start-up templates, but one of the oldest and most well-known is the Business Model Canvas, developed by Alex Osterwalder. You can search the web to find free templates of the Business Model Canvas, or other versions, to build your business plan.

These are the nine basic components of the Business Model Canvas version to integrate into the business plan text.

1. **Key partnerships**
   Note the other businesses or services you'll work with to run your business. Think about suppliers, manufacturers, subcontractors, and similar strategic partners.
2. **Key activities**
   List the ways your business will gain a competitive advantage. Highlight things like selling direct to consumers or using technology to tap into the sharing economy.

3. Key resources

List any resource you'll leverage to create value for your customer. Your most important assets could include staff, capital, or intellectual property. Don't forget to leverage business resources that might be available to women, veterans, Native Americans, and HUB Zone businesses.

4. Value proposition

Make a clear and compelling statement about the unique value your company brings to the market.

5. Customer relationships

Describe how customers will interact with your business. Is it automated or personal? In person or online? Think through the customer experience from start to finish.

6. Customer segments

Be specific when you name your target market. Your business won't be for everybody, so it's important to have a clear sense of who your business will serve.

7. Channels

List the most important ways you'll talk to your customers. Most businesses use a mix of channels and optimize them over time.

8. Cost structure

Will your company focus on reducing cost or maximizing value? Define your strategy, then list the most significant costs you'll face pursuing it.

9. Revenue streams

Explain how your company will actually make money. Some examples are direct sales of products, fees for services, membership fees representing special benefits, and sponsoring events for which an attendance fee is charged. If your company has multiple revenue streams, list them all.

Traditional Business Plan

You might prefer a traditional business plan format if you're very detail oriented, want a comprehensive plan, or plan to request financing from traditional sources.

When you write your business plan, you don't have to stick to the exact business plan outline. Instead, use the sections from those described here that make the most sense for your business and your needs. Traditional business plans use some combination of the nine sections noted previously.

Appendix

Use your appendix to provide supporting documents or other materials that were specially requested. Common items to include are credit histories, resumes, product pictures, letters of reference, licenses, permits, patents, legal documents, and other contracts.

Business Plan Assistance

Assistance in writing your business plan is available from several nationwide sources. You can contact SCORE, a confidential business advice provided by a network of 10,000 volunteer business experts; Small Business Development Center, Women's Business Center, or Veterans Business Outreach Center.

Now that you have reviewed all of the information provided by the SBA, here is an example of a basic business plan for a small business, a beauty salon called The Studio. This is to allow you to have an understanding of the general layout.

THE STUDIO
BUSINESS PLAN

Prepared by
Jane Doe

123 Waterfront Blvd
Philadelphia, Pennsylvania 19130
555-555-5555
Style@thestudio.com
www.Thestudio.com

I. Executive Summary

The Studio (referred to from hereon in as the "Company") is intended to be established as a Limited Liability Company at 123 Waterfront Blvd, Philadelphia, Pennsylvania 19130, with the expectation of rapid expansion in the salon and barbershop industry. The Company solicits financial backing in order to be able to introduce its new service (described in the following).

Business Description—The Company shall be formed as Limited Liability Company under Pennsylvania state laws and headed by Jane Doe.

Jane Doe has over 20 years of experience in the salon industry. She has created a team of experts that are passionate about their craft as well as providing an excellent experience.

The Company will employ eight full-time employees and three part-time employees.

Management Team

The Company has assembled an experienced management team:

Studio Coordinator—*John Doe—With 10 years of experience John has demonstrated exceptional leadership qualities and is an inspirational motivator.*

Business Mission

The Studio will provide a safe, comfortable, and creative space to allow for excellent service in all things for hair.

New service:
The Company is prepared to introduce the following service to the market:
Salon and barbering: The Studio provides a variety of salon and barbering services. Specializing in haircutting, barbering, color, keratin, and extensions for all hair types.

Funding Request

The Company requests a total loan of $150,000 over the course of five years, to be used for the following purposes:

Funding will be used for cost of business build out and set up as well as marketing and staffing.

Purpose	Loan Amount
Marketing and promotion	$50,000
Staffing	$50,000
Construction	$50,000
Total:	$150,000

Long-term debt payment is a key feature of the Company's financial plan. We expect to break even within a two years' time period following the introduction of our service. Financial predictions suggest a minimum 50 percent return on investment by the conclusion of the financing period.

II. Business Summary

Industry Overview

In the United States, the salon and barbershop industry is estimated at $57 billion. Current totals indicate 75,000 beauty salons generating $47 billion in revenue, while 20,000 barber shops nationwide account for $20 billion in sales.

Research shows that operators in this industry focus on short- and long-term factors when making operational decisions such as the following:

Business Goals and Objectives

Short term:
To achieve a 50 percent return on initial investment within two years while continuously hiring and expanding our team.

Long term:
Open additional locations once the business has made a return on my investment and the business is consistently profitable.

Legal Issues

The Company affirms that its promoters have acquired all legally required trademarks and patents.

III. Marketing Summary

Target Markets

The Company's major target markets are as follows:

- Target market is both a male and female demographic of all ages.
- Advertising with gear to ages 25 to 55 and within a 10-mile radius.
- The estimated number of potential clients within the Company's geographic scope is 10,000.

Promotional Strategy

The Company will promote sales using the following methods:

- Online marketing through a variety of social media platforms.
- Signage advertising and print advertisements.
- Referral incentive program for new and existing clients.

Competition

In the salon and barbershop industry, customers make choices based upon:

- The level of competition is nearby hair salons and barbershops.
- The business's reputation and quality of work.
- The primary competitors for the business are the following chains: The Hair Cutter and Sports Clips.

However, we believe that the Company has the following competitive advantages: We offer a family-owned business that supports the community through sponsorships and events.

Services

First-rate service is intended to be the focus of the Company and a cornerstone of the brand's success. All clients will receive conscientious, one-on-one, timely service in all capacities, be they transactions, conflicts, or resolution of complaints. This is expected to create a loyal brand following and return business.

IV. Financial Plan

12-Month Profit and Loss Projection

Monthly expense for salaries and overhead (projected): $40,000
Revenue and sales for first year of business (projected): $2,000,000
Gross profit for first year of business (projected): $200,000

Questions

1. What type of business do you want to open?

_____

_____

_____

2. Why is this type of business your business of choice?

_____

_____

_____

3. Approximately how much funding would you require to start up?

_____

_____

_____

4. What is the average salary of someone in your industry of choice?

_____

_____

_____

Journal

What did you take from this chapter?

_____

_____

_____

_____

_____

CHAPTER 4

Cribs

Figure 4 Real estate adventures

Photo: Peeterv/iStock by Getty Images

Let's start with the business of property ownership otherwise known as real estate investments. This is a common business that people from all walks of life try to get into. All you need is money, good credit, and thick skin. We all need to thicken up our skin because that is what it takes in business practices. This goes for most business investments. Nothing comes without taking a risk. But in the real estate world there are many things that can come up both before and after the transaction.

Some people are extremely successful in real estate investments, and some people are not so lucky. Here are some things to think about when investing in property as an individual or a partner.

- The first one is very simple. What's the plan?
- Literally, why are you investing in property?

- Are you doing it because you know someone that does and they are seemingly successful? Seemingly is the key word there.
- Perception of success can be a true disillusion. Do you want to give up your day job and make real estate your new career?
- Is it a side gig and you'd ideally like to flip a few houses and put some cash in the bank for that trip around the world you've always wanted to take or perhaps for your retirement?
- Maybe you need to double your money to try to pay your kids college tuition that you weren't able to save for because life got in the way.

Whatever the reason, you need to know first and foremost you're taking a risk. So before you throw the dice down that craps table of flipping a house, make sure you have your estimated budget and multiply that number by two. If you really want to play it safe, multiply that number and time frame by three. In most situations of rehabs, new construction, and even basic projects, it runs over time and over budget. So do not believe Mr. Contractor when he says it will be done in two months because it won't. This is usually hard lesson learned.

So let's figure out your goals.

- Do you want to flip houses?
- Do you want to rent and be a landlord?
- Do you want to buy land and build on it?
- Do you want to buy an existing structure and rehab it?
- Do you want to convert a church to condos?
- Do you want to own a duplex perhaps, rent one and live in one?
- Do you want to manage a multiunit apartment building or deal with commercial space?

We have so many options here.

Let's tiptoe behind the scenes for a moment. Did you take the time to look into the land rights? Land rights, you ask. What are land rights?

Well for starters, there are two different kinds of *Land Rights*, surface and subsurface.

You have *Surface Rights*, which are the rights to access the surface of the real estate. This covers both natural elements and structures, from trees to buildings, what's obviously on the surface.

Then you have *Subsurface Rights*. This is regarding all that is found beneath the surface of the land. It applies downward to the center of the Earth. This can apply to drilling oil or minerals of the earth. You discovered a gold mine underneath your pool that you decided to take down; you better hope that you own the Subsurface Rights or your gold mine just vanished.

OK, so you look into this and find out that you are in the clear. There are not any restrictions on the surface or subsurface of the real estate that you're interested in. (Thank goodness, you struck gold!)

Have you looked into the forces of nature issue? Is there accretion, erosion, or reliction happening in the area in your new potential investment? Is avulsion a possibility? Unless you're an attorney, a developer or a real estate agent you have most likely not heard of three out of four of these terms. So let's do a quick review.

- Reliction—A gradual increase in land area when water gradually withdraws.
- Avulsion—Sudden loss of land by a flood of some sort.
- Accretion—A gradual increase of land area potentially by deposits of soil.
- Erosion—Gradual loss of land overtime. We often hear this phrase along the coastal beaches.

Now let's discuss some of the economic characteristics of the land. These characteristics are equally as important as any when deciding where to invest and to determine if this area is a perfect fit for your plan.

The terms Scarcity, Situs, Fixity, Illiquidity, and Modification are all things that should be considered before making your investment and taking a risk in developing your business in this industry.

- *Scarcity.* When the supply of land is limited or scarce. The supply of land will not increase but the demand to live there will. This applies to city living. From rowhomes to high-rise condos, city living packs people in without providing a lot of land for them to own.

- *Situs.* The economic importance of a property's significance or where the property is located. The cheap, abandoned, overgrown lot with a beautiful view of the park just may be a total score!
- *Modification.* When the value of the land can be affected due to the changes done to the property. An upgraded kitchen with high-end appliances and marble countertops is a common example of a housing modification. Modifications such as kitchens and bathrooms are an investment that will increase the value of the property, so if you're going to put the time and money into it be sure to do it right and don't cut too many corners.
- *Fixity.* The fact that real estate exists in a fixed location and can't be moved.
- *Illiquidity.* The relative difficulty of converting an asset to cash without loss of value.

These things are necessary to factor in order to understand the potential of your investment.

It is very important to know what is included within the real and tangible property of the real estate. In addition to the land rights, be sure to have a full understanding of what the water rights are if you are near water. *Air rights* are another thing to think about, particularly if you're planning on building up.

There are endless situations where real estate transactions go bad. This is where you want to make sure you have a good real estate agent and/or attorney.

Some other things to think about when it comes to real estate investing are as follows:

Ok, so you determine that you want to invest in rental properties.

What type of property are you looking to purchase? Single family, duplex or a multicomplex are some options. Always check *the zoning*. A property may be set up as a business but may not be zoned that way or vice versa. In today's day and age of community associations, you best believe that someone is watching and paying close attention to building sales and the future intention of the space. Personally speaking, I never could quite grasp why your neighbors have a right to say what you do with your investment. I have witnessed neighbors freaking out about abandoned lots that were disgusting and dangerous. It was home to drug addicts leaving needles and broken bottles all around. Cars would constantly be broken in there and it was a nuisance area. An investor wanted to turn the lot into a beautiful gated safe parking lot with landscaping that would add overall value to the neighborhood. The neighbors screamed and fought about it in the community meetings. It eventually happened, but it was drug out for two years. And this was just a parking lot improvement project.

Let's say that Uncle Bob has a duplex that he wants to sell, because he took another teaching job that he has to relocate for. You and your buddy have been talking about making a real estate investment. You both decide to meet Uncle Bob for coffee one morning to talk about this potential business venture. Everything sounds great. The rental income history is good, the taxes on the property and insurance costs are feasible based on the rental income and Uncle Bob is going to give you a discount on the property sale. Bonus!

Uncle Bob brags about what great shape the building is in, and you believe him. Why wouldn't you? After all, it is Uncle Bob and besides that the building looks pristine. The outside looks immaculate and manicured and the inside is freshly painted and the appliances look new. Overall, it looks like it's in great shape. Should you really spend $600 on an inspection? YES!

*NEVER SKIP THE INSPECTION!

An inspection is a necessity no matter what anyone tells you. After your formal inspection is complete, you will have a much better understanding of what maintenance the property is in need of. Depending on the square footage of the property the inspection cost will range. This is money worth spending to protect yourself. Keep in mind that codes change for a reason. Safety is always a priority. Having a property properly inspected gives you an idea of what level of financial investment you are getting involved it. Even if it's trusty old Uncle Bob's duplex that has been seemingly well maintained over the years.

Actually, you want to get that inspection especially if it's Uncle Bob's place. You don't want to get that discounted sale price from Uncle Bob and then find out afterward that the entire electrical system has to get ripped out because it is a major fire hazard.

You haven't been aware that Uncle Bob himself has been doing all the maintenance over the years and he's not an electrician. But he is a professor at the local college and does have a master's degree in history. He just doesn't want to pay an electrician to do something that he can do himself, so he watched some tutorials and rewired his entire property. It does not recommend messing with electricity unless you are an expert. To rewire a lamp is one thing. To rewire a house is a whole other ball game. So when the light in the dining room continues to flicker and again when the kitchen outlets don't work, and then the hallway shorts out, he fixes it. He watched some YouTube videos and did the electrical work himself. And there is nothing wrong with that, kudos Uncle Bob! It is quite applaudable for him to take this on. But just make sure you get the professional home inspection or there's a possibility that you can be coming out of pocket an easy $15,000 later, with a bonus price of some serious legal and family drama.

If you prefer to avoid drama, you're getting that inspection. After you get your inspection report, be sure to get estimates on the work needed. The report may or may not give you some estimated costs of repairs, but just take the time to get your own estimates. Three estimates are typically the recommended number of estimates that you should get. It gives you a solid comparison. Even if you know somewhat about residential plumbing and are planning on doing some of the work yourself, take some time and have a few professionals come in to look at the jobs needed. This will allow you to have more perspective of the level of work that will need to happen.

Now you have your inspection report and you got your estimates. It's time for you and you best buddy to do the math and figure out if you want to do this.

The property cost $X.
The taxes equal $X.
The necessary modifications cost $X.
The insurance costs $X.
The total equals $X.

But don't panic, because you already know that Uncle Bob has been renting both of his units for the past 10 years and the rental income is enough to cover all of these costs and make a decent little profit.

But is the profit worth it? Is the effort, financial risk, time, and energy worth the amount of money that will be left over each month? Don't forget you want to save up and build a nest egg for a rainy day otherwise known as the day that the heater or central AC unit ceases to operate and has to be replaced. This is just some things to think about.

Investors

Now you know what you're in for, financially at least. It is time for you and your best pal to sort out the investment strategy.

Typically, there are two types of investors. Capital investors and sweat equity investors.

Capital investors are those that put up capital otherwise known as making a monetary contribution. They take a lot of risk. Some capital investors are involved on the front lines of the project and some are folks that are risk takers that go in as silent investors but have nothing to do with day-to-day operations.

Then you have those that put in *sweat equity*. This means putting in time and energy instead of capital. There is really not much financial risk involved as a sweat equity investor. The biggest risk is wasting that time and energy. Aside from that, you didn't put any money out of your pocket so if things go wrong it is no financial loss to you.

Part of the problem with sweat equity investors versus capital investors is that sweat equity investors can eventually lose interest and motivation. This is because it usually takes years to start making any money back. There's something very motivating about having financial skin in the game.

In the beginning stages of the investment project, everyone is super excited to be a part of something new and potentially awesome! Those that put up the capital are excited to get that rush when they start seeing the return on their investment, or even just getting the money back that they originally put out, but again that takes time.

Sweat equity investors are excited to see the reward for their blood, sweat, and tears. For some, this is a wonderful opportunity for them because they just don't have the money to do something that they want to be a part of. They are motivated and eager to do their part.

I can't stress enough that in most cases it takes some serious time for all investors of any kind to start making money, let alone making their initial investment back. That being said, sweat equity investors can seemingly work for nothing until the company starts to generate revenue. Unless they have negotiated themselves a salary with the company. Sometimes that is feasible and sometimes it is not. It really depends on the functionality of the business.

Sweat equity investors can feel like they are working for free. They are the ones putting their time into the project. For example, they may be handling the management and labor aspect and dealing with the day-to-day grind while waiting to make some money. Now we already know they have no upfront financial risk because they put up no capital. When you don't have any risk and you are sick of "working for free," you can easily get frustrated and lose interest in a project. That's when things can get ugly. This same situation applies to most businesses, really. It could be a disaster waiting to happen. So be sure that you are all prepared and properly informed and have a realistic timeline as to when your business could possibly be profitable.

Here's a Story About Ralph and Marty

Ralph is just starting out his career in the financial world. He is in the beginning phase so he has extra time on his hands because he is not that busy. He doesn't have much money because he's just starting out. Marty is an accountant. He had been in the business for a while so he's a pretty busy guy, having less time under his belt. He also has some cash available that he would like to invest. They both want to put their eggs in different baskets and invest in different things. The problem for Ralph is that Ralph doesn't have any extra eggs lying around. Marty's issue is that he doesn't have the time to invest. Let's do the math here: Marty's eggs plus Ralph's time equals a potential partnership having a nice balance of two people who want to diversify and invest into something. After a few chats, the two of them work out a plan that Marty is going to put up all of the eggs otherwise known as capital. He is going to continue to work in his accounting job. Ralph, on the other hand, isn't going make any monetary contribution, instead he has plenty of time to oversee the potential investment project and will be investing his time and labor. This is otherwise known as sweat equity.

The two of them decide to make a go of it. They do their due diligence, research, and make a plan as to what area they want to purchase, factoring situs, and scarcity.

They decide that they want to go in as long-term investors and rent the property out. They can be landlords, right? Anyone can be a landlord. Sure, no problem.

To ensure they don't have issues collecting rent, they decided to rent to the city's low-income housing department. In doing so they get paid directly from the city and there will be no issues collecting money from the city or so one would think. That is a whole other story.

Marty goes and gets the proper certifications needed to rent to this particular organization through the city and they get things moving. They realize that with Ralph having no capital to contribute the amount that Marty can contribute won't be enough to purchase the house and cover the costs of the necessary updates and repairs.

The two of them realize that in order to make this work they are going to need more capital. They have a few options. They can try to take out a mortgage on the property and then take out a construction loan to cover the cost of the modifications. Another option is they will need another capital contributor. Given their plan they didn't want to have to take a mortgage out, just yet. And they didn't want to just give up so easily. So they did some investigating and went on a search for investors.

Turns out they know a guy, named Ray. This particular guy may be interested in investing. They go to Ray and present to him their plan. Ray has some extra money in the bank and tends to be a risk taker, so he decided to get involved.

This is when all the fun starts and things get formalized. They form their company, create their operating agreement, and buy their first house. They knew that the house they were buying needed work, it was obviously in pretty bad shape. Because they saw the work that needed to be done they decided not to waste money on getting an inspection, Rephrase, they made the mistake of not getting an inspection. Ugh! Ladies and gentlemen, always get the inspection! What you see isn't always what you get. Sometimes it's much worse.

So fast forward, they end up having to put in THOUSANDS of extra dollars more than they planned for into renovating the house. There was leaky plumbing and mold that needed to be addressed. We know Ralph doesn't have this money, and Ray and Marty already put up the money amount that they felt comfortable with in the initial planning phase, and they didn't want to take out personal loans or tap into personal funds. But somebody had to.

So, to keep things flowing, Marty puts up more money. Great! Thanks Marty. Things get moving. The house gets rented and everyone is good.

Then they decide to take a mortgage out on the house. They were able to do so because they increased the value of it by fixing it up and showing income from the renters. They find a small credit union to fund them. With this mortgage, they are able to pay themselves back some of the capital and take the extra money to put toward another house. Sweet!

This time they add in another risk taker to the crew. Ralph brings in another investor that he has a relationship with. This guy has some extra money and wants to invest with them. He shares the same interest of Marty and Ralph and would like to put his eggs in different baskets.

They got the inspection done and they were able to purchase the house outright. They fixed up the house but ran into some issues with the contractors not making deadlines and taking forever to get the jobs done. The contractors are Ralph's friends and his contribution to this investment is making sure these things are getting done in time and on budget. Hiring friends to do the work makes things awkward and especially when the work isn't getting done. But eventually and over budget (again) it got done and they got renters in this house.

This went on for several more houses and different partners in the mix. Ralph's real job in finance had become very busy, so the houses and tenants became an annoyance for him to manage. And each time Ralph managed to never put up any capital. He would just find other capital investors, buy and fix up another house and then take out another mortgage. Again they had to put in more money than expected into fixing up the house and so on. Which was all fine and dandy until the properties and their tenants were too much for Ralph to deal with. So at the end of each lease, the tenants would move out.

After the tenants moved out, the repairs that were required would cost a whole lot of money. The cost of repairs outweighed the amount of income that these houses had generated. Because of this, five out of the six properties became vacant, because no one wanted to put any more time or money into these houses. Here's the thing, vacant properties can't pay the mortgages. Vacant properties can't pay the taxes and the insurance does not pay itself either. So what happens then? They decided to sell the properties. If only it were that easy.

Two years went by. Marty's wife, Jane, started asking about what was going on with their housing investments. Ralph and Marty who were once good friends have been avoiding each other like the plague. She asked her husband what was going on and he gave her a brief summary, giving his side of the story.

Jane then picked up the phone and called Ralph. They had been friends since childhood and she wanted to know what his version of the story was. Their friendship became distant and he just kind of fell off the face of the earth, and Marty's wife wanted to know if something else was going on. They had been so excited to get into business together.

They had a genuine conversation. He gave his side of the story. The common factor was that they were both very frustrated with the situation and because of that they became frustrated with each other. None of the partners wanted to put any more time or money into these properties. They had put them up for sale and there were no offers made that could work. They stayed vacant for years. They would have had to take a significant loss on all of the properties in order to pay off the mortgages with the few offers that they did get. In addition, they would all have lost all of the initial monetary investment.

No one was putting up any more money for the repairs and all of the investors became angry with the situation, each other and they all just stopped communication. The houses remained empty. It was a nightmare situation.

During the conversation between Jane and Ralph, Jane listened to Ralph's frustration as well as experiencing frustration first hand with her family's finances. She offered to help. Ralph accepted her offer in disbelief that it would even be possible that she could help them out of this nightmare. She promised to help and made it a goal. After all, her and her husband had been floating a portion of the expenses since none of the investors would contribute any more money. But the taxes and insurance still had to get paid and obviously with multiple vacant properties they don't get paid on their own.

She reached out to anyone that would listen and pitched the portfolio of the four houses. She showed the properties countless times. They were disgusting, dirty, abandoned houses. They were gross, but she continued to show them.

Needless to say Jane was ticked off that they had been paying for the houses out of their personal finances and no one else had even given a thought to how these bills were being paid, let alone made a contribution to the overhead of these vacant properties. So she insisted that Marty have a meeting between the investors, give them an update and made sure they all informed and held responsible their share of the costs. He was resistant putting a meeting together and would rather continue to deal with the headaches then deal with the partners. It didn't matter that all of the investors had made it clear that they would not put any more time or money into these houses or there was now bad blood between them. This is business and that is just not how it works.

Jane insisted. She couldn't understand how her husband made it comfortable for them by just deciding to handle all of the bills. They knew the houses weren't rented, yet they never inquired about the mortgages, taxes, and the insurance were being paid. Quite the opposite actually, they started spreading lies about Marty making it out to sound like he was getting over on them. When in reality Marty was trying to avoid foreclosure so he was doing what he had to do to make sure it didn't affect anyone's finances or credit, even when it meant that he was the one paying for it.

Finally, after many months and many showings, Jane found a buyer. She met the investor and showed him the properties and with some negotiating a deal was made. When Marty contacted the other investors to let them know that they had an offer on all of the properties, suddenly their attitudes changed. They changed in the opposite direction that you would expect. Instead of being relieved and happy that the headache was over, they now wanted to keep the properties. Marty told them that they would have to buy him out if they wanted to keep the properties. He had been dealing with them while no one else was and no longer wanted to be involved in a partnership group in which consisted of partners that didn't take responsibility for the properties outside of the initial investment cost. The partners still did not want to put in any more money to fix up the houses or pay the bills, let alone buy Marty out. They had every right to make this decision. There is no rule that partners have to continuously contribute capital. This often is where people and business run into problems.

Ralph encouraged her to help in the beginning. He even told Marty to give her a finder's fee as an incentive for her to get them sold. Then when she finds a buyer for the portfolio of all four properties, Ralph asks her to stay out of it! Talk about creating bad blood, at the end of the day, her and her husband's money was paying for these properties. It affected their personal finances. It shows up on their combined tax returns. Financially they, as a married unit, are financially involved. Besides, even after the houses were listed unsuccessfully with multiple different realtors, she was the one that sold all four houses in one combined portfolio for them. She is not a realtor, so she did not receive one cent. Previously Ralph agreed to a finder's fee if she was able to sell any one of them let alone all four. That changed quickly and not only did she not get a finder's fee for the sale, there was not even a thank you from the investors. Needless to say, their friendship was officially tarnished.

Now not all investments end up being this bad. There are plenty of investors that have a great amount of success. But these things happen. So before you get involved make sure you have a plan in place as to how your partnership should end, before it begins. It will come to an end at some point, have a professional help you plan for the exit.

Questions

1. Would you consider getting into business with your friends? Why? Why not?

_____

_____

_____

2. Is real estate something that you would want to invest in? Why? Why not?

_____

_____

_____

3. What could the investors have done to avoid this situation?

_____

_____

_____

4. What type of professional would you go to before making an investment decision?

_____

_____

_____

Journal

What did you take from this chapter?

_____

_____

_____

_____

_____

CHAPTER 5

Wise Guys

Figure 5 How to make wise decisions in forming your entity

Photo: Serpeblu/iStock by Getty Images

Deciding the structure of your company is a decision that you need to choose wisely. You want to legally separate yourself from your business. Now the question is what kind of entity should you form ... and why? The decision of forming a partnership, a Limited Liability Corporation (LLC), an S Corp, or a C Corp, or just being a sole proprietor can be a little overwhelming. It's important to know and truly understand the difference. So let's do our homework on this one.

Limited Liability Corporation

LLC members are protected against liability. They are not liable for company losses or company debts and it's a way to protect their personal assets. LLC members do not have to have formal meetings and they can choose any form of profit distribution.

Pass through taxation applies and the company itself is not responsible for paying taxes unless it chooses to be treated like a corporation. All taxable income applies to its members. It's a relaxed way to protect an individual from its company without all of the high-strung legal mumbo jumbo, with the exception of loans and leases.

An LLC cannot go public and is usually dissolved when a member dies or the company is facing bankruptcy.

This happens, people! I can't stress this enough, always think about the end when having your operating agreement drawn up. When I ask people what their exit plan is and they say things like, "Why would we put an exit plan in place? That's like saying it's going to fail." Uhhhh no, actually it's saying that when it comes to an end, you are prepared. It's like people who are offended by a prenuptial agreement. I know we don't like thinking or talking about negative possibilities, but unfortunately, we live in a land called reality and these things happen.

Sole Proprietorship

This is pretty common for start-ups with one person, hence the sole part of the title. It's probably the easiest formation. Record keeping isn't super strict and you can avoid double taxation. You get all the risks and benefits of running an enterprise. It's pretty clear and simple for a one person show that doesn't plan on bringing in shareholders or partners.

C Corporation

An attractive way to form a company that would have multiple people involved is forming a C Corp. Shareholders, stocks, strict record keeping, and formal meetings are necessary for operations. Shareholders can be extended to foreign nationals and the number of stockholders can be unlimited. The company lives until it is purposely dissolved.

A C Corp offers a lot of protection to its owners keeping their assets protected. However, there are exceptions to that, but you would have to be silly to put yourself in a position where you're not personally protected. For example, be sure to deposit taxes deducted from employee wages. And don't purposely punch someone in the face with the intention of hurting them, no matter how badly they may deserve it. Avoid doing things that will get you in trouble and open you up to legal action.

S Corporation

Like a C Corp, an S Corp offers the ability to have shareholders and stock options. However, it is limited to one type of stock and less than 100 shareholders.

There is no corporate tax and there is a reduction on capital gains. Shareholders pay taxes on all profits per calendar year, even if those profits are not distributed. You can only use domestic capitalization. So if this sounds like what's in your plan then go get your company set up as an S Corp.

Consulting with a professional to have your entity set up is the way to go. You can speak with an accountant or with an attorney and make an educated decision as to the best option that makes the most sense for your business goals.

Questions

1. Name one difference between a C Corporation and an S Corporation.

   _____

   _____

   _____

2. What two types of companies that you would you like to be a part of? Why these companies?

   _____

   _____

   _____

3. What type of business entity would best suit both of your business choices listed previously.

   _____

   _____

   _____

4. Why would this be the best option for these businesses?

   _____

   _____

   _____

5. What type of professional would you consult to help set up your corporation?

   _____

   _____

   _____

Journal

What did you take from this chapter?

_____

_____

_____

_____

_____

CHAPTER 6

Hangry for Business

Figure 6 The restaurant biz

Photo: Gorodenkoff/iStock by Getty Images

For those of you who think that I spelled hungry incorrectly, I didn't. Hangry means angry or irritable as a result of hunger. It typically relates to actual food hunger, but in this case it relates to business hunger. And sometimes being hangry can make you do irrational things in order to be fulfilled.

We all love bars and restaurants. I know I do and I know that my friends and family do as well. To go into a buzzing bar or restaurant has such good energy, well at least it that was the case pre-COVID-19 and it will be again someday.

Picture this, you just enjoyed a delicious meal and you may have had a specialty cocktail or three. You had an overall great experience. You look around and people are talking, laughing, and having a good time. You see old friends sitting at the bar and go over to say hello. Families gathered around a table. There is a large group of friends making a toast and celebrating something special. Everyone is really enjoying themselves.

You may start to think that it looks like a fun business to run. Perhaps you envision yourself owning a bar or restaurant someday. And one day this very type of opportunity may knock at your door. Before you jump in to the restaurant business, you should have a conversation with multiple restaurant owners and hear about what it entails. Owning and operating a restaurant is not a job, it's a life.

The Adam Story

Adam lives in Washington, DC. He has a gorgeous home there in a desirable part of the city. He is a very successful, educated, respected man in the political scene. He is also someone who is a risk taker. He is often hungry for new investment opportunities. He has a beautiful second home in Virginal Beach. He spends a lot of time there. He loves to frequent bars and restaurants. After all, he is a successful single guy.

Well, one of his friends from the beach introduces him to a couple who owns a seemingly successful bar/restaurant in the beach town not far from where Adam's place is. It's a couple towns over and lately the town is booming! New development is constant and the town itself is vibrant and alive. The couple is looking for an investor to come in as a partner and help them revive the restaurant. Adam is always up for a new business venture, so he was intrigued. He visualized himself surrounded by friends having a great time. In his mind, he saw every seat filled in his swanky buzzing restaurant. Cha-Ching!

Adam has a formal meeting with the couple in their beautiful restaurant space. They have been running the restaurant for several years already, and this year the business took a turn. They explained to Adam that the former manager mismanaged the place and they are looking for investors to reestablish and rebrand. They do not own the bricks. I repeat, they do not own the bricks, so they are renting the building. They did an excellent job painting a vison for him to see the potential. They took Adam's interest to a whole other level. The space itself was already in great shape and created a vision that sounded even better. They were able to really peak his interest.

Adam has a great resume. From his fancy education to his job history, Adam has a large network of friends. Many of them making the big bucks, and himself included. He is very handsome and charming.

He pretty much has it all going on. He was an ideal investor for them. He had money and a large network of friends who are successful as well. They would be happy to support Adam's new restaurant. Adam was very appealing to the couple, as a matter of fact he was exactly what they were looking for ... and more.

Adam goes to his cousin, Christian. He tells Christian all about this new venture and asks Christian if he wants in. Basically, the two cousins would go in as silent partners and Janice, who is the wife of the restaurant owner duo, would manage the restaurant. Janice's husband was hands off in running the daily business operations. He had a career that really consumed his time, and besides this was his wife's dream that he was being supportive of.

Christian talks to his wife about this exciting new business opportunity. He tells her everything he knows about the proposal and he wants them to invest a lump sum of their money into this place. She had one very important question for her husband. Why do the owners need investors if they have owned and operated the restaurant for several years already? He explained that it was due to poor management. He told her that they had hired a manager previously and he did a bad job of managing and was stealing from the business. His wife asked what would make the management better this time around. Christian explained that Janice herself was going to manage the operation, instead of outsourcing a manager. Because this is her business, she will make sure it is done correctly and she will be on top of everything.

Not Going to Happen

"Does this couple have any children?" Christian tells his wife that they have five children. "How old are these children? If they are ages 21 and up that's great, they can help market the place." But no, they are all under 12 years old. "Nope, not going to happen," she replies. She gave the thumbs down to this investment opportunity.

Christian was very upset with his wife's dismissal of this investment opportunity. He went over the business proposal, the vision for each floor of the restaurant ranging from a sports bar to a wine bar to employing a top-notch chef.

His wife was not budging on her mindset. The potential sounded amazing. The place was beautiful in a great location. But all of that didn't matter. It did not matter what amazing things were going to happen inside that space to make it look stunning. The fact that overshadows it all is that the manager of this bar/restaurant is a mother of five young children. This 24/7 project can never be her baby, it's that simple.

But Christian and his cousin went through with the investment anyway. They blew through all of the capital within six months. They redesigned the layout and hired a new staff. They had a mixed marketing plan to accommodate the vibes of the place. They advertised the hottest DJs for late night dancing, marketing their wine bar specials. They highlighted their talented chef and his beautiful delicious food creations. They did everything they could to bring people in.

A few months went by and Janice was burned out. She was tired of being there all the time. She asked her partners if they could help with management. They both helped as much as they could, but managing is not what they signed up for. They wanted to protect their investment so they did what they had to do to pitch in and help out. Things were still a struggle and the restaurant was failing. So six months later they decided to rebrand again.

Adam asked Christian to put up more capital to keep the place going. Christian thought about it but his wife was still angry about the first lump sum that they put up. If he put up more of their money, she was going to lose her mind, and likely end their marriage. He decided not to invest any more.

Adam, on the other hand, continued dumping his money into it. This went on until there was no money left to dump. He cleared out his personal savings and tapped in to all of his funds. He was determined to save the restaurant and have it be successful. Sadly, he eventually had to file for bankruptcy himself. Later that year, the business closed down. Christian lost his capital investment and Adam lost every cent that he had saved, trying to keep this place going. He was so hangry for this business to succeed that he made poor investment decisions.

When investing into a bar or restaurant or any business really, it is critical to look past the books. Look past the numbers that you are presented. Look past the vision. You have to look into the person in charge of running the business. If that person is motivated, focused, and driven, chances are you are taking a safe risk. If there are obvious priorities in that person's life, then chances are it's not worth the risk. Janice is a mom of five small children. She was a housewife who was looking to a purpose other than her children. The bar/restaurant never stood a chance. Plenty of men and women have a very successful work/home–life balance. It most certainly depends on the individual's personal circumstances and work ethic. But operating a bar/restaurant is more than a career, it is a life. It is far beyond a nine-to-five job schedule. It is late night operating hours and early morning food pickups and deliveries. It is a grind like no other.

Questions

1. What could Janice have done differently to be a successful bar/
restaurant owner?

_____

_____

_____

2. Would you consider investing in or owning a bar or restaurant?
Why/Why not?

_____

_____

_____

3. Why do you think Janice chose to go to private investors instead of
taking out a small business loan?

_____

_____

_____

4. At what point would it make sense for you to walk away from an
investment?

_____

_____

_____

Journal

What did you take from this chapter?

_____

_____

_____

_____

_____

CHAPTER 7

Rooted

Figure 7 Family business

Photo: Monkeybusinessimages/iStock by Getty Images

There are a lot of service-based businesses out there to get involved in. Service business models require a decent amount of manpower. From operating a nail salon to owning a painting company, finding dependable, trustworthy, and trained employees is necessary. It is also a lot harder than it sounds. Like any business, you can create the most beautiful space known to man but if you don't have the right people involved, then your investment can be snipped.

Sally and Her Mom

Sally worked at a hair studio with her mom. Her mom had owned three studios for 45 years and Sally's been working for her for about 15 of those years. Sally recently joined her mom as a business partner, so the business was changed from a sole proprietorship to S Corporation. Sally's buy-in to the company was a little bit complicated, and here's why.

Sally's mom had a seemingly successful business, but she wasn't the best at handling finances. Luckily, she owned the bricks. And even more luckily for her, the building that she purchased 45 years ago was in an area that gentrified and was now very desirable. The neighborhood that the building was in led to an increase in property value over the years. This gave Sally's mom an opportunity to use the building as collateral for loans.

Sally's mom was able to refinance her building several times over the years. Each time she took money out on the property, and it allowed for her to continue her business operation. These loans made her mortgage payments increase throughout the years. This financial structure worked out well for years, until it didn't. In addition to her most recent mortgage, she took out an interest-only line of credit.

One of the problems with interest-only credit line is that she didn't realize that her payments didn't go toward the principle and she only paid the interest. The other problem was that the interest rate fluctuated, which caused her payment amount requirements to be inconsistent and essentially increase from month-to-month and over time. Year after year she paid the amount that her monthly bill balance was, but it never deducted money from the principal balance. Again, this was because the payments only covered the interest. Payments continued and the loan stayed the same, and she never noticed. This is being repeated because when taking loans and mortgages out you should always pay close attention to the loan structure or you can get yourself into a lot of trouble.

Sally's Mom's Finances

Sally's mom didn't have a full understanding of her loan structure. She trusted one of her clients whom she worked with to take out a line of credit. But she didn't take the time to really read through the paperwork to get a clear understanding of what she was getting into. And it was never explained to her, or maybe it was and she didn't pay attention. Either way after years of payments, she didn't realize that her loan amount never decreased on this particular loan. It wasn't until one day that Sally's mother came to Sally for help again.

Sally's mother came to Sally several times and needed to borrow money. She explained to Sally that she couldn't afford her mortgage payments. Sally couldn't understand how this could be. She knew that her mom bought the building 45 years ago. She would have thought that the building was paid off, since most people stick with a 30-year mortgage or less, but instead it was quite the opposite.

Sally asked her mom to sit with her one day after work. She told her to bring her check book ledger and a copy of all of her bills. As they went through all of the bills, Sally in a very old school manor wrote down all of the bill amounts. On a sheet of paper, she jotted down the amount for her mom's car payment, insurance payments, utilities, student loan payments for her sister's college loan, mortgage, and the credit line costs. She approximated the cost of food, clothes, and a few bucks for extra activities. Then she wrote down her mom's income number, ultimately creating a hand-written profit and loss statement.

Off the bat, it was obvious to her that the debt-to-income ratio was not working out. On a scale from 1 to 10, Sally's mom's income was at an annual rate of $60,000 and she needed a $100,000 to afford her lifestyle, which wasn't very lavish, by the way. That's a problem. So how do you decrease your debt and/or increase your income? Let's find out.

The simplest way to decrease debt is to decrease your spending. No more fancy coffee stops in the morning, time to make your own coffee. The nail salon every two weeks will have to get stretched to once a month. Weekly car washes now become monthly car washes. Season tickets to your favorite sports team, well it's time to sell them off. The point is that there are a lot of ways to increase your money, just by making lifestyle changes.

With her mom's approval, Sally took the time to call the mortgage company as well as the bank that the credit line was through. She asked questions about how to go about paying off the loans. She was able to put in place a payment plan that would start effectively paying the principle of the loans down. But that still didn't touch the fact that she wasn't making enough money to cover all of this cost. Even by cutting costs there was too much of a difference.

Sally thought about it. She told her mom that the only way to fill the gap was to generate more income. But how do you just magically generate more income? You don't. In business, there is no magical way of getting new customers or selling anything. It takes time, planning, and it takes another level of work.

In this case, Sally understood the business and she knew that she could help her mom generate more income and pay off the debt. She also knew that it would take some time, money, grit, and perseverance.

After thinking long and hard about it, she made a business proposal to her mom.

She said that she (Sally) would take a significant pay cut, she would invest capital into the building in order to add more stations, recruit and train new staff members, and handle all of the business finances. If the plan works, then Sally and her mother would use all of the additional income to pay down the debt owed. In return, this would be her buy into the business. Sally's mom agreed. Besides Sally's mother was over 70 years old and really didn't have the desire or energy to do it herself. Sally's mom told Sally that if this plan works and her debt is paid off, she can then take over the business in full.

For years, Sally thought about going out on her own and starting her own business. She didn't have the heart to leave her mom. Now that she had a clear understanding of how bad her mom's financial situation was, she decided to step up and help her. Sally did inform her older brother about what was going on with their mom. She asked him if he wanted to get involved and help his mother out and help pay down her debt or contribute to the plan. He declined. He told Sally that they all have known just how bad their mother was with money and that her finances are not his problem. Sally and her mother proceeded with their plan.

They had a partnership agreement drawn up and the fun began. Sally expanded the business by reconstructing every inch of usable space. She bought additional furniture, upgraded the electric and plumbing for the additional stations, up graded the air conditioning to accommodate the increase in heat, she put new windows throughout the building, and then had the entire building painted. Sally made a capital investment as well as put in sweat equity.

She started actively recruiting and training new talent. She put together and executed a marketing plan to bring in new clients. She expanded their service list and she worked behind the chair herself tirelessly for years, even after she took a significant pay cut.

Well, guess what happened … it worked! The team grew, the salon got busier and there was an increase in revenue. The business itself took on the mortgage and loan payments, leaving Sally's mom with financial breathing room. And when all was said and done, Sally's mom signed the business over to her daughter. She continued to work and make money, yet she relieved herself of all the bills, overhead, and headaches of dealing with everything. At that point, she was over 75 years old and happy to be done with all of it.

Questions

1. Try to apply some ways to decrease your debt and increase your income specific to the industry that you are interested in.

   _____

   _____

   _____

2. Would you take a financial hit to try to help your family members business? Why/Why not?

   _____

   _____

   _____

3. Would you allow someone else to take a financial hit to help your business if you were unable to do it on your own? Why/Why not?

   _____

   _____

   _____

4. What would you do to avoid this predicament?

   _____

   _____

   _____

Journal

What did you take from this chapter?

_____

_____

_____

_____

_____

CHAPTER 8

Can You Hack It?

Figure 8 Think you got what it takes to be a boss

Photo: IgorIgorevich/iStock by Getty Images

We heard about Sally's successful business plan coming to life. It's nice to hear when success happens. It's not all bad, but you have to take the bad with the good in business. So let's stick with Sally's journey for a bit and we can take a sneak peak in to the growth of the salon. Put hold on to your hats kids, this gets a little juicy!

One day, Sally gets a call from her younger cousin Jenny, who is also a hair stylist. Jenny was very upset on the other end of the phone. She was telling Sally how she hated the current salon she had been working in and that she left there. She had been part of a team who walked out from her previous salon and was promised a chair at the new salon if she went with them. But they kept her on as assistant until her boss thought she was ready to have her own chair. That day didn't come fast enough for Jenny, so she up and quit. She heard about the expansion of her aunt's and cousin's salon so she called cousin Sally inquiring about a job opportunity.

In true loyal family fashion, Sally hired Jenny even though it didn't quite sit right that she admitted to being a part of a walkout and knowingly screwed over one boss by leaving with some other team members. Then quit in the middle of a busy Saturday with another boss. Those two scenarios were alarming to Sally. Jenny admittedly screwed over her past two bosses. She painted herself as the victim because she did not get her way.

But they weren't her family, so she would never do anything like that to her own cousin and aunt. Sally hired Jenny.

About five years later, Jenny had a nice growing book at the salon. She was doing well and it was nice to see. Sally had coached and mentored her to the best of her ability. They traveled to do education sessions together, had drinks after work, and their families and kids spent a lot of time together as well. They had really bonded and became very close.

In the meantime, Sally had another business opportunity with a friend of hers. Sally's friend Melissa had been asking Sally for years to open a hair studio with her. Melissa always wanted to leave the salon that she was in and own a salon herself. However, she wasn't prepared to do it alone. She wanted a partner, and what better partner than her old friend Sally.

Sally had three kids. Her oldest was in high school, middle in elementary, and her youngest was a toddler. Melissa had three kids also. They were a bit older though, two in college and one in high school.

Sally was willing to help Melissa from the sidelines but didn't want to go all in because she already felt stretched thin. She was managing her and her mom's salon along with being a mom and taking care of her kids. Melissa begged and begged Sally to join her. Sally felt her curiosity starting to kick in. She talked about it with her husband and he was supportive. After doing her due diligence and planning out each of their roles in the business, Sally finally agreed to partner with Melissa.

They formed a Limited Liability Corporation and had their partnership agreement drawn up by an attorney friend of Melissa's. They each were going to start off with a $20,000 capital contribution. Melissa and her husband stopped by Sally's house and along with their husbands to pop champagne to celebrate this exciting new chapter.

Together they begin planning. The lease signing was scheduled for a Monday. The Sunday evening before the big signing, Melissa told Sally that she was going to come by her house. She did. As she entered Sally's kitchen, Sally knew something was wrong. Melissa broke into tears. She started freaking out and then basically had a mental breakdown in the middle of Sally's kitchen. She backed out of the partnership agreement.

Sally was stunned and confused. Melissa had begged her to do this with her and now she is the one backing out. It didn't make sense to her. But after putting time and energy into all the planning, Sally had gotten excited about this new business venture.

Sally decided to go through with the business without Melissa as a partner. Melissa said that she still wanted to come and work for her, but she didn't want to be a boss. Sally let her out of a $20,000 partnership agreement.

A short time after, the build-out of the new salon was almost complete. A week before the salon was scheduled to open Sally and Melissa met for coffee. Melissa told Sally that she will not be joining her in the new hair salon. She was going to stay at the salon she had been working at. Needless to say their friendship was done. As the saying goes "Screw me once, shame on you, screw me twice shame on me."

Hindsight is always 20/20. When Sally thought back she should have known that Melissa couldn't hack it as a business owner. She used to talk poorly about a colleague of hers calling her a work robot, because all she did was work. In the meantime, Melissa never worked more than a 20-hour work week. The money she made was just her spending money, because her husband took care of all of the family's finances. She did not have a strong work ethic; she just had a temporary notion that she wanted to be a boss. When things became real the thought of having to really work and dedicate her time freaked her out and scared her off.

Sally could have held her accountable for her $20,000 capital contribution, but then she would have had to deal with this unstable business partner for the duration of the business. It was just not worth it. Besides, Sally didn't ever want to speak to Melissa again. Their relationship was over.

Questions

1. What were some of the red flags that Sally should have paid attention to?

_____

_____

_____

2. What do you think Sally and Melissa could have done differently to avoid this from happening?

_____

_____

_____

3. Why do you think Melissa felt so strongly that she wanted to own a business and then when the opportunity was put in front of her, she backed out?

_____

_____

_____

4. Do you think Sally should have gone ahead and opened the business anyway? Why? Why not?

_____

_____

_____

Journal

What did you take from this chapter?

_____

_____

_____

_____

CHAPTER 9

A Wolf in Sheep's Clothing

Figure 9 Betrayed in business

Photo: David Roberts/iStock by Getty Images

In business and in life, you have to beware of the wolves in sheep's clothing. Have you ever heard of this phrase? A wolf in sheep's clothing refers to someone who may appear harmless, but they have a dangerous and ruthless nature just waiting to come out. They may be really good at hiding it, but it eventually shows itself. Beware of the wolves because they appear when you least expect it.

Being in business is about making money. When people see an opportunity to get in on the action and make themselves some moo-lah, you best believe they are going to do whatever they have to do to get in on the action. Of course, they will present themselves in the nicest possible light and then when they see the opportunity to bite off their piece of the pie or eat the entire pie themselves, you better look out! That sweet little lamb just may be a big bad wolf.

You know Sally from Chapters 7 and 8. She really had a taste of doing business, both a sweet and sour taste. She has experienced a successful outcome in one business and a complete burn in another business. But she kept plugging along between both businesses. It was exhausting but she was determined to make the best of it.

In the meantime, Jenny was in a difficult situation herself. This is where it gets a little crazy. Jenny's husband, Donald, was under a federal investigation. He was a union worker who would go to nonunion job sites and sabotage their work. He was caught by an illegal wiretap that was put on some of the phones of the local union leaders. The Federal Bureau of Investigation had camera footage as well but couldn't positively identify each of the guys involved because they would do their dirty work at night.

They knew who these guys were because of the wiretaps, but the wiretaps were illegal so they were not admissible in court. Some juicy stuff here kids! The Feds nicely came knocking on Jenny's door wanting to chat with her husband.

Needless to say, he was scared. He knew he was guilty but he certainly didn't want to go to jail. He talked to his uncle who was an attorney and he talked to a friend who was also an attorney. He was trying to get advice as to what to do. He knew that it was him in the videos. He knew that it was him on the wiretap. He was freaking out because he was looking at serious jail time in a federal prison.

Jenny went to her older cousin Sally and told her everything in the meantime, it was all over the news, so it was no secret. Then she asked if she could be a partner in Sally's new hair studio. Sally did not have a good feeling about this. But she realized that her cousin was going to be in a really bad position if her husband went to jail. Sally let her family loyalty override her gut feeling and agreed to take Jenny on as a business partner.

Jenny and Donald had children and her salary alone wasn't enough to cover their lifestyle. Jenny was never really much of a worker. She complained about how tired she was, about how her feet hurt or her back hurt, or she was too busy or she was too slow. She was just a complainer, and in a princess kind of way. She was late for work all the time and she left early at every chance she got. She lacked drive and grit. That was OK because that worked for her. It worked for her because her husband paid all of their bills. Her paycheck was just her personal shopping money. She didn't have to work, let alone work hard.

Sally used poor judgment based on loyalty to her family, and together they had a partnership agreement drawn up at a heavily discounted rate. Even though Sally's spouse thought it was a bad idea, Sally let Jenny buy into the business. They were now equal business partners at one of Sally's studio locations. But Jenny was still an employee at the other location, where she continued to work for her cousin and her aunt.

When Sally first decided to open up the new studio she had previously set a financial plan to NOT take a paycheck for the first year of working there. This was in order to build up cash as an attempt to get her capital investment back in the first 12 months. She had taken a loan out for and invested it into the studio. The amount was $40,000 (which she had let her previous partner out of $20,000) and worked at that location without pay for the first year, while still working at her other studio. She also hired multiple employees with hopes of generating income. She went one year without a paycheck from one job but continued to work two jobs. So when Jenny came in as a partner, part of the agreement was for her to not take a paycheck until the end of the same 12-month period, which at that point was at six months in. Jenny agreed to not take a paycheck for her first six months. Then at the end of the year they would see how much money the company made and they could each take a drawl accordingly.

Investing in Jenny

Jenny only put up a small fraction of capital in comparison to Sally's initial investment. Even though her contribution as a whole was lower, yet she was given the opportunity of a 50/50 partnership. That was a huge mistake on Sally's part, she really wanted to help her younger cousin, but screwed herself financially in the process. She knew she was taking a "haircut," but she made the decision anyway in hopes that it would incentivize Jenny to work harder so that their business could be successful.

As it turned out, Sally found out that it was nice to have a likeminded business partner. They divided up some of the job duties. She had another set of eyes and hands in dealing with new staff members. In the meantime, they both still worked at the other location as well, in which they were able to collect a paycheck from. By hiring a staff and splitting their time, this ensured that Sally's business with her mom would be kept going and they could get paid from their time there as they were both very busy with an existing client base. Sally worked tirelessly between both locations.

Jenny had an unrealistic budget for changes and upgrades that she wanted to make at the new salon. For example, she wanted to order a custom-made $5,000 reception desk. They didn't even have a receptionist. Jenny's product orders were over-the-top expensive, leaving them with lots of expenses and thousands of dollars in unnecessary retail just sitting on the shelves and in boxes collecting dust. Sally had to pull Jenny back in on spending. Quite frankly, she was shocked at her spending desires and capabilities. Jenny and Sally had to discuss and agree on large purchases before they were made. After all this was a brand-new business, and business was very slow in the beginning. Jenny never experienced having financial responsibilities or having a budget. With her husband handling all of her finances, she had no clue about spending do's and don'ts.

*So far the point of this story is to make sure you have budgets, roles, and responsibilities spelled out beforehand. This will help to avoid overspending and going outside of what the business can afford, as well as creating an uncomfortable situation that could ultimately be detrimental to the business and a partnership.

Sally taught Jenny all about the business side of things. She learned about the daily operations behind the scenes, instead of running the business in addition to client interaction of just behind the chair. From scheduling to payroll to marketing, they covered it all. She taught her how to efficiently order retail and supplies within a reasonable budget. Jenny finally had a true understanding of how the business operated.

In the meantime, Jenny's husband got a get out of jail free card. He did not have to go to jail after all. He decided to rat out his friends and save himself. He cooperated with the Feds while his friends stayed tight lipped. He sent them to jail and he got to stay a free man.

*Note: Unions are important to society. They help provide jobs in safe environments and ensure fair wages.

Back in the day there was a union mindset in some of the trade unions. It was like a code that only union employees should be hired to do work. This generally applies to large jobs, because the union workers felt that their wages and requirements were fair. Not everyone agreed to that. So companies would hire trades people outside of the union. That makes the union angry and, in some cases, they would retaliate in a harmful way. In reality, anyone and any business has the right to hire whomever they chose to do work for them. To harass other company owners, their employees, their family members, and their customers is wrong. To harass and sabotage them just because they shopped around and got a better price or have an in-house team that is not part of the local union is illegal. It is one thing to stand outside a construction site with a giant blowup rat, it's another thing to harass and intimidate people because they didn't pick you for their services. Everybody shops around for everything. Hence the three estimates theory. Besides, why do you think companies offer coupons? It's to attract people with lower pricing.

Now to play devil's advocate, a lot of times the companies that go outside of the union will hire nonunion tradespeople or hire nonunion companies that hire tradespeople under the table. Meaning they will pay the workers cash and they do not report taxable income. So basically, they are hiring cheaper labor and paying them less than union requirements and the laborers do not have to report the income and can charge cheaper rates. This avoids good old Uncle Sam crushing them in taxes like the legitimate workers are hit with.

All that being said, both these situations are illegal. But in the age of technology, intimidation and harassment are easier to track than cash exchanges and the Feds have a field day with these things. The Internal Revenue Service is the one that has fun with the tax evasion. And at the end of the day they both can lead to prison.

So where were we? About four months after Jenny and Sally's partnership began, Jenny started talking about opening another location. Sally was all for it, but the timing wasn't right at the moment. She had just worked for eight months and not collected a paycheck for the current company, let alone to see a penny of her initial capital contribution. She wanted to get some return before she jumped to something else.

She wasn't quite ready yet. She suggested waiting until the end of the year, so they could assess their financial situation better. It was only a few more months before the end of the first year at the new business. But Jenny wanted to make a move and open another location immediately. She had every right to do so. Sally was just not ready to be involved in another business. She let Jenny know that and Jenny started to get very distant.

One day while she was at the studio Jenny called all of her clients from the first location and asked them to come to the new location as she would only be operating out of there. She up and quit overnight working for her aunt and her cousin. She never even had a conversation with them about it. Then she took action against the new location. She took down the salon's social media pages. Running the social media was her responsibility and she was in charge of it. She closed it down, deleted all the posts and pictures of the entire team, and then told their employees and clients that Sally was closing the studio and kicking her out of the business.

She internally tried to sabotage the business, but why? One of the team members saw what was happening when Sally wasn't there. She was upset and confided in Sally about all the negative things Jenny was saying and doing. She was intentionally creating a negative and toxic work environment. Two of the employees quit because Jenny told them that the salon was closing and to find other jobs before it closed. There was another stylist who was about to start working there and Jenny told her not to come to work there as well. Sally was head spun and so was her mother!

Jenny reached out to Sally to set up a meeting so that they could discuss what was happening. During the meeting, Jenny admitted that she purposely tried to sabotage the business, because she was mad at Sally for forming a professional relationship with her former employer. She then went on to tell Sally that she hated her former boss. This came as a shock to Sally. It had always appeared that Jenny idolized her former boss. Sally was so baffled by hearing this. She had no idea that this was even a thing. Jenny was also angry that Sally wouldn't agree to poach employees from their uncle's salon. It really showed that Jenny was not someone she could have as a business partner. It was too little, too late at this point. What do you do when your business partner tries to sabotage your business?

In the meantime, Jenny and her husband went and opened another salon. They tried to poach employees from both of Sally's locations. They successfully poached the two cousins from their uncle's salon, ultimately screwing their uncle over and causing major drama and heartache. But wolves don't care about that. They are ruthless.

Jenny had a vision. She wanted to own her own salon in a specific location. Jenny knew what she had to do. She knew that she would look bad if she blatantly screwed her cousin and aunt over, since everyone knew that Sally and her mom were the ones who took Jenny in and gave her a job when she asked them to. Sally mentored her and then gave her the opportunity to be a business owner. So, Jenny created a narrative, so that she could leave the salon and make her cousin sound like a monster, all while making herself look like an innocent little sheep. She acted as a wolf in sheep's clothing. Her plan worked like a charm!

She made Sally sound like a bad person and she was made out to be this poor little thing who just had to escape this monster. She told lies to the clients, in which the other team members witnessed. She created a toxic environment for everyone there. She really went all out. She even convinced her husband's uncle to make up a lawsuit against Sally. It was completely based on lies and severe distortions of the truth. Nothing ever came out of a lawsuit full of lies.

*This is where emotional intelligence comes into play. As a business owner you cannot act with your emotions. Business partnerships are not like a teenage relationship quarrel, where you cheat and deliberately try to hurt the other person and then get back together. If you mess with your business partner at the level, it usually doesn't end well. If something makes you angry or upset, you have to take a moment to truly evaluate the situation. Take a breath and understand that your words and actions are going to have an effect. What does a business partnership break up mean? It typically doesn't end when you don't start out with an end plan. It can often end in a lawsuit.

Family Interventions

Uncle Paul who was a lawyer and he knew about all of the illegal activity that his nephew was involved in. This was the same uncle who coached his nephew into ratting out his friends so that he didn't have to go to jail and sent his friends to jail instead. Jenny and Donald even convinced

Uncle Paul to put up the capital so that they could open another salon, in return offering him a partnership. So Uncle Paul now had a vested interest in them and their new business, which means he had a vested interest in trying to get money from cousin Sally. He fronted them the money and was willing to do what it took to get his capital back so he played along and composed a frivolous lawsuit to try to get what he could. Sally was caught off guard by the fabricated accusations within this lawsuit. She was incredibly taken back because the accusations that were made were the things that Jenny herself did. Even when the easiest thing to do was to give them money just to go away, Sally new that this was so incredibly messed up, so she would not concede.

Working with family can be difficult. If you do, make sure you don't do any favors and if you get involved with family members or friends be sure to put everything in writing. Sally clearly has a problem with giving chances to those whom she shouldn't give chances to. Starting out in business you can't be blinded by the optimistic vision of the future. This is extremely unfortunate, but it's true. You have to put your emotions aside and think clearly. You have to evaluate people's work ethic, drive, and business mindset.

Sally should have never gone into business with Jenny because she felt bad for her. She knew Jenny was a lazy worker. She also became aware that she was fine with her husband's criminal activity because it funded her lifestyle. Sally was not blind to that, but she put her loyalty to her family first.

If you are going to have business partners make sure they are like-minded, driven, and motivated. When dealing with family members, friends, or anyone at all in business it is crucial to document everything. Every single cent should be documented as well as everyone's roles and expectations. Most importantly, be sure to have an exit plan. All things must come to an end, both good and bad. By establishing these goals and expectations in writing you are creating a clear shared vision between all parties involved.

Questions

1. What action(s) could have been taken in the beginning to avoid any drama?

_____

_____

_____

2. Do you think this partnership could have been repaired? Why/ Why not?

_____

_____

_____

3. What should have been done in the beginning of the partnership to help avoid this drama?

_____

_____

_____

4. Do you think that it is OK to poach employees from another business? Why/Why not?

_____

_____

_____

Journal

What did you take from this chapter?

_____

_____

_____

_____

_____

CHAPTER 10

Loyal Till the End

Figure 10 *Noncompete*

Photo: William_Potter/iStock by Getty Images

A noncompete document is an agreement where one party agrees not to start or enter another business that will directly compete with a specific business or industry. There are specific parameters that are listed. They do have to be within a reasonable distance and time frame of leaving your previous job in order for it to hold up. It is both business savvy and street smart.

The document title is self-explanatory. An employee will not compete with the employer who is providing them with a specific job opportunity. This type of agreement is smart to put into place in industries involving sales and services.

In most service and sales-based businesses, individuals are given insight and tools. They are educated and mentored and eventually given the opportunity to grow a client base. Great, that's what we want. So, as the owner of the company, we make sure they have all the resources that are needed in order to do just that. From marketing, to education to supplies, these business building tools come out of the business. And that is otherwise known as the business owner's pocket. The owner of the company is basically making an investment in their employees and hoping to get a return on that investment. It is generally set up to protect the legitimate interests of a business. Examples of such businesses are such as, but not limited to, medical providers, salespeople, service providers, accountants, and lawyers. Virtually every type of business can be protected through a noncompete.

The noncompete document has become a necessary part of protecting business structures. If your business does not have a noncompete in place with your employees, you really should consider getting one.

You don't want to invest tons of time, money, and energy into an employee who is going to take, take, take ... and then roll out and open up their own shop down the block essentially becoming direct competition. How can you avoid this from happening? Well for starters, you can present each new hire with a noncompete agreement. It can specify a distance in which they cannot operate out of within a reasonable amount of time. This type of agreement is standard throughout many industries.

Luke's Gym

Let's take Luke for example. Luke just opened a brand new, state-of-the-art gym. Luke saved up all the money he could. He took out a small business loan and he got things rolling. Exciting, right! Yes, it is, because it takes a lot of nerve to take this kind of risk!

Luke recruited some of his good friends to come in as personal trainers. He helped them get their certifications and cultivated them. While he encouraged them to have a personal style, he personally coached them to enhance the overall client experience. This provided a universal style of training for his company's brand. He watched his business grow. One of his buddies in particular was very motivated and successful.

Tony had built an incredible client base. His social media presence stood out and he quickly gained lots of followers. He even started a side gig running senior citizen workout camps outside of the gym. Tony even had Luke and some of the other trainers help him with the senior camps.

Luke was happy to support his friend. The senior camps that Tony started were not competition with his gym and it was a great way to support the community. Seeing how serious Tony was about his profession, Luke really helped promote Tony both in the gym and for his outside camps. They worked so well together and really lifted each other up. They had a very unique and inspiring friendship and professional relationship.

What Luke didn't do was have Tony or any of the other staff members sign a noncompete. Luke was friends with all of these guys and especially Tony. They were best friends. Luke had nothing to worry about with any of them. They would never betray him and leave the business that built them. Luke felt strongly about how loyal they were and he was just as loyal to them. He would do anything for these guys and vice versa … so he thought.

Then one day Luke started noticing a difference in Tony's social media posts. They were all about contacting him directly for training and not mentioning the gym at all. Luke asked Tony to remember to promote the gym as well when posting. Cross-promoting is an important tool in the platform of social media marketing. Tony said he would and acted like it was just an oversight on his part. The two friends continued on working together because there was no issue. Tony just had made a few mistakes by not cross-promoting the gym. No biggie.

*Promoting is crucial to the success of your business. Having your team and your clients and other businesses promote the business will inspire positivity and growth. Back in the day, the best type of business promotion was by word of mouth. That still is effective but cross-promoting is hands down the most effective because it reaches so many people/potential clients. The same thing goes for them. When you and your business promote them, it helps to build them and improve their image.

A week later, Luke found out that Tony was getting ready to open his own gym. He set up a gym right down the street. It literally was only two blocks away. Tony told Luke that he was leaving. He explained to Luke that he wanted his own business. Off he went to open it. He had contacted as many clients as he could and tried to recruit them to leave Luke's gym and come to his gym. Luke was blindsided completely. Not to mention, he was pretty hurt by this, both financially and emotionally.

Now this could have been avoided. If Luke gave all of his employees a noncompete he could have protected his business from being depleted of clients quickly and unexpectedly. That is such a hard thing to bounce back from. No matter what the relationship is, do not run your business based on the idealism of loyalty and friendship. Employee's will come and go. It does not have to be a negative thing for your business. It can often be a proud moment to watch an employee fly off to do their own thing. It is the way that it's done that makes or breaks the situation. So do yourself a favor and get past the awkwardness and make sure *everyone* signs a noncompete.

Questions

1. What are your thoughts on a noncompete agreement?

   _____

   _____

   _____

2. Why do you think Tony didn't let Luke know about his plan to open a gym two blocks away?

   _____

   _____

   _____

3. If Luke did tell Tony about his plan to start his own business do you think they could have worked together and collaborated? Why? Why not?

   _____

   _____

   _____

4. If you were asked to sign a noncompete from an employer would you? Why? Why not?

   _____

   _____

   _____

Journal

What did you take from this chapter?

_____

_____

_____

_____

_____

CHAPTER 11

Mentorship

Figure 11 Managing your employees

Original Art by Chris Redmon, BPES

A great mentor is able to recognize and then inspire the greatness in those whom they are mentoring. It's not about making someone more like you, it's about making them the best possible version of themselves.

Get to know your mentee. Inquire about their life outside of work while keeping professional boundaries. This will help provide you with insight as to who they are. It will also let them know that you recognize them as a person not just as a mentee or employee. Ask them to share some information about themselves.

The following are some questions that you can ask them:

What led you into this career?
What do you like about it so far?
What is not your favorite part so far?
What is your story?
What stresses you out?
What is your outlet?
What are your hobbies?
What's your favorite food?

These are all topics that we all can relate to. It's a nice opportunity to get you both at a level playing field as humans.

Now that you got to know a little bit about your mentee it's a perfect time to establishing ground rules. Make it known that these rules are firm and they are not meant to be bent or broken.

For example: In the salon/barbershop industry, it is common for there to be a territorial mindset when it comes to clients seeing another stylist or barber.

That's My Client

Here's a story about Jenna.

Jenna is a hairstylist at a men's hair salon called Salon for Men. She has been building her clientele and has a nice repeat clientele.

One day Jenna called out sick. All of Jenna's clients were contacted and offered the opportunity to reschedule with Jenna. Most of them did reschedule with her. But John was going out of town and really needed his haircut, so he asked if anyone else was available that day.

Salon for Men was able to accommodate John and schedule him with Liana. It worked out great. John was very happy to be able to get in and was also very impressed with his experience with Liana.

A month later, John went online to book his next appointment. He noticed that Liana and Jenna both had availability. The timing that Liana had worked a little better for his schedule that day, so he went ahead and booked with her.

John went in for his cut. Jenna was with another client so he wasn't able to say hello. Halfway through his haircut Jenna noticed that it was "her client" John laughing in Liana's chair. Jenna excused herself from her guest and walked over to Liana and John. John said, "Hey Jenna, it's good to see you." Jenna angrily replied, "What are you doing? Why are you in her chair?" John and Liana and everyone else around them were shocked! John awkwardly replied, "The time she had available worked better with my schedule today." She stormed off and went back to what she was doing.

Liana apologized to John. She was cringing that Jenna just put John in such an uncomfortable situation. John blew it off like it was no big deal. When he finished paying for his haircut he said goodbye to Jenna and Liana.

They never saw him again.

Because Jenna acted unprofessional and possessive toward John, she made him never want to go back there again. He chose to find another place to go for his service. So Liana, Jenna, and the salon lost a client.

This situation should have been handled completely differently. Jenna should have said hello to John and let him know that she's happy to see him. At that point, John would have felt comfortable coming back to either one of them and everyone would have been comfortable and happy.

One of the ground rules that I set with my mentees is that we share clients. Knowing that the "That's my client"/client possession mentality is a common industry mindset, the fact that it is not acceptable in my studio is a clear boundary that I set from day one. I teach them that they should absolutely be grateful to their loyal clients, while being understanding that we all have busy lives and sometimes our schedules do not sync. They are coached to make their loyal clients feel comfortable if they have to "cheat" on them once in a while. This promotes overall brand loyalty as well as respect between team members and guests.

It is always a bonus when there is an organic connection between you as the mentor and your mentee. That allows for a smoother transition and immediately cuts through any possible awkwardness that can sometimes exist in the beginning of a relationship.

That's not always the case. If there isn't immediate professional chemistry, it's totally fine as well. It may take a little more time to try to get in tune with each other. That in and of itself, is a lesson to be learned. It's a genuine demonstration of how even though you're not necessarily each other's work soulmates, you can be professional and have a respectful relationship. This is a wonderful lesson in dealing with clients and colleagues.

Not everyone is going to have the same views and opinions. As long as they share professionalism in the workplace, that's what is important. It literally comes down to respect and understanding that in life and in work you can agree to disagree. However, you are in the position of leadership and authority and with that comes an expected level of respect. If there is too much disagreeing happening, then that can be an issue that needs to be nipped.

Keep your cynicism low key while allowing your constructive criticism come through as a teaching moment. It's OK to provide constructive criticism. In these moments, you can offer a solution and explain why trying this approach is more beneficial in this particular situation.

Showing Appreciation

Allow your optimism to shine brightly! Take the time to complement their performance. Show appreciation and make it known that you value their effort. Ask for your mentee's opinion as to how they would approach a specific situation. Allow them to have a voice and let it be heard.

Acknowledging your mentee's accomplishments can be very uplifting to them. When you watch them set goals, working toward these goals and execute them is a sign of focus and determination. It is so satisfying to both of you to see an organized effort come into play. You definitely want to take the time to acknowledge it.

Hard work can come in different forms and in different situations. Personally speaking, if a team member or members gets positive feedback from a guest I will send a message to our team highlighting those who are involved. I try to encourage everyone to join in and it becomes a fun and positive experience. It's awesome when your peers become your hype people. I also send pictures of positive reviews to share with our team. This also encourages positive feedback.

When an individual works hard toward a personal goal, I like to really give them individual attention. It can range from a phone call, a text message, or a one-on-one meeting. It becomes like a proud parent moment. To me, it genuinely feels that way. I want my mentee to know that I see how hard they worked or how they stepped out of their comfort zone to reach a goal.

It is motivating to have your accomplishments acknowledged. It feels good. When something feels good, it becomes an experience for which we try to continuously strive.

If a mentee or team member works hard consistently and is never recognized, are they going to stop working hard? Probably not, but they will always appreciate positive reinforcement. As a mentor, you can't go wrong with it. It will stimulate and motivate your team.

Applying Insight

When the situation calls for it, provide guidance and direction based on the insight that you have gained around a situation or those involved. Sometimes it may point in a direction of something completely different from when you started together. It happens that way sometimes. It is OK to support redirection if need be. We all have something to learn. Always remember that you may know a lot and have a lot to teach, but there is always something to learn no matter how many accomplishments you as the mentor may have under your belt.

In the modern day, the workplace has shifted in a very different direction. Workers today usually start out grateful, but they quickly begin to think about what's next. What's better? What's more exciting? What's going to pay me more? What job can I do less work and make more money? Employees want to know what you, as the employer, are going to offer them.

When an employee lands the job they desperately want, they are excited and motivated. They give it their all. Then after a while, after they've put in some time, establish a role in the company and start to feel comfortable with their position, they start to see themselves as valuable in your company, and that's usually where something shifts in them. They may get a little cocky or full of themselves.

There can be a mindset that starts to make a mentee or employee overvalue themselves. Typically, you can see it happening. Their behavior starts to change. You may see them get less motivated. You may see their energy decrease, or their appearance change. They may start to show up late, or just on time versus the early person they used to be. Keep in mind, they are reading motivational books and listening to podcasts about how they can do anything if they put their mind to it. They are thinking about what they don't have in their current position. The grass is always greener on the other side ... or is it? In reality it's green where you water it.

That's when it's your time to make an important leadership decision. For starters, you can have a one-on-one meeting or a light conversation with them and do a check in. That's if you want to have a chance of keeping them around for a while longer. Sit them down, have a compassionate conversation and see what's going on with them, ask how they are doing, and just try to figure out what's up. Show empathy and understanding. It's a great time to make a plan on how to reset their goals and stimulate their motivation that has been lying dormant for a bit.

The second option is to simply let them drift away and wait for them to leave. Sometimes it's just their time to move on. It doesn't have to be a bad thing. But it's nice when an employee leaves on good terms. You can still have that one-on-one and check in with them, but if their mind set and goals are set in a direction that your company can't help them with, then it may just be best for you to wish them good luck in their new adventure.

Then there is the self-destruct mode. They will self-destruct if they don't know how to make a change. Sometimes this happens when a person feels stuck. Emotional intelligence applies to both sides of the spectrum in a job setting, both with leaders and with employees. So when an employee can't figure out a way to leave they may act out. They may start to spread venom within the company and create a narrative, so that when they leave a perfectly good it is justified. This creates a toxic environment. Try to get ahead of that. Have that one-on-one and let them know it's OK to move on. It will help keep the environment drama free or at least drama reduced.

I've seen it all. Realistically, there are some people who I have been really disappointed to see leave, but they had reasons that I couldn't compete with, as their employer. Rather than becoming upset, or being annoyed, I was genuinely happy for them.

There were some employees who left to pursue other opportunities and it was like a giant weight being lifted. They created a toxic environment. That is, bashing the business, bashing the leadership, coaching other employees to leave the company, and brainwashing clients to believe lies so the clients would not come back to the business after this employee left. They may want to destroy your business.

Why would someone that you mentored want to destroy your business? The most popular reason is because they have a personal agenda. They may be planning or starting their own business or joining on another business that may be competitive to yours, or they may be envious of your role, or they simply may not like you. Obviously, they don't want to look bad. So they paint a picture of this horrible company that they had to escape from. They start their own business and recruit as many clients of yours that they can. For these types of employees there is no changing direction. They have an agenda. So pay attention, get ahead of them, and let them go.

As a mentor, it is important to get to understand your employees and learn what approach to take with each individual. A blanket approach is fine, but you will get further with a customized approach. Use your emotional intelligence to figure out your coaching strategy. And if you don't know how to access that internally, there are plenty of classes and literature available that will truly work with you to improve your techniques. This is what makes a leader stand out. Going the extra mile to work on yourself and your leadership skills are sure to help you be a successful and effective leader and mentor.

Questions

1. Who is the mentor who has left a positive impression on you?

   _____

   _____

   _____

2. What is something that you learned by reading this that you never gave thought to before?

   _____

   _____

   _____

3. Do you see yourself being a good mentor?

   _____

   _____

   _____

4. What would you add to your list of questions while getting to learn about your mentee.

   _____

   _____

   _____

Journal

What did you take from this chapter?

_____

_____

_____

_____

_____

CHAPTER 12

The Big Mahoff

Figure 12 Image is everything

Photo: PeopleImages/iStock by Getty Images

If you are wondering what a Mahoff is, let alone a big one, don't worry because I'm going to explain it to you. Does it come in small? Nope. There are two different types of a Mahoff. Generally speaking, a Mahoff is someone of power, money, and prestige, and sometimes a Mahoff has none of that but they act like they have it all. They can also tend to come across as having a matching ego. Often the higher ups of corporations can be considered the big Mahoff. Presidents, CEOs, and CFOs are a few examples of who would be considered a Mahoff in the corporate setting. In a community or neighborhood setting, the Mahoff is the guy who buys the whole bar rounds of drinks, the person who always picks up the bill, the go to for money, loans, or donations. A Mahoff is basically someone of a generous nature who can come off as flashy. When you're the Mahoff of your crowd, everyone knows it. It's a beautiful thing to be a generous and giving person. But you have to beware because when people know you're of a giving nature, you may become a target. A target of whom or what you may be thinking. A Mahoff can become the target of the takers. As much as there are givers, there are those who latch on and take advantage of their generous nature, even in business. A Mahoff may be easily lured into investing into a seemingly potential successful business simply by dangling a seemingly good opportunity in front of them. This brings us to mergers and acquisitions.

An acquisition is when one company purchases or obtains all or another company's shares. This allows them to gain control of said company while keeping the same name and legal entity. Typically, the intention of acquiring a company is to essentially better the company. Figuring out the strengths and weaknesses of that company will allow it to grow, ultimately generating a profit for the buyer within time.

A merger describes two companies uniting. After the merger is complete, one of the companies is dissolved and is basically absorbed by the other company.

Mitchell's Story

Mitchell is an entrepreneur who has recently gotten involved in multiple companies. He has personally bought out multiple businesses of different natures. His companies have been part of different mergers and acquisitions. He's the guy who does things big. He has money to spend and likes to share the wealth, and he enjoys helping people both in business and personally. He often picks up the check for the entire table at dinner with friends. He makes large donations to local charities. Overall, he is very generous. He does all of these wonderful things for others truly expecting nothing in return. Because he is more generous than most people in his circle, he comes across as the big Mahoff.

As mentioned, Mitchell owns several companies. Ironically, he was not out looking to buy any companies. He had his own start-up that he was quite busy with. So how does Mitchell come across these acquisition opportunities? Well, by his friends and acquaintances, of course. They know that Mitchell has money that he throws around. At first, it's nice.

Then it's impressive and then it's just too much. At that point he becomes looked at differently. That's when he becomes known as the Mahoff.

One of Mitchell's friends made an introduction between Mitchell and his buddy Eric. The other intro was made by a different friend of his.

(Note: Friends and family members in business may not the best combo, if you haven't picked up in that one already. Always tread cautiously and document everything in the process.)

One of the acquisition opportunities was a painting company and the other was a landscaping company. They both were attractive. Both have contracts with big name corporations, developers, and huge job projects generating lots of money. Why would a company that is busy and generating lots of money want to sell? There are many reasons, but we are going to focus on the one that is within our control if we get ahead of it. Cash flow is one of the most important things that an inexperienced business owner may overlook. Generating money and collecting payment are two different ball games, so you have to be prepared financially to cover the business expenses as well as your personal expenses without receiving payment for an extended period of time after a job is complete, in certain industries.

At a commercial level in both of these industries, it is common to not collect payment until at least 30 days, after the job is done. That means you have to take all of the upfront supply costs and labor costs into consideration before accepting a job. So you have to have enough money accessible to pay for all of it, do the job, and then wait months for payments. This is not ideal.

It actually is kind of nuts that there isn't a collaborative effort to put some of the upfront cost on the client in certain industries. The issue seems to be that the market is so saturated with competitors that these companies would rather continuously take out loans, credit lines, and tread water than try to build some of the upfront cost into the initial client contract. I have seen some larger chain corporations take to this, but small business owners are hesitant to do so because it is not a universal practice and they may not get the job if they attempt to negotiate upfront payment. My suggestion would be to try it. Then you can just negotiate from there if it doesn't work out immediately. With the process of construction loans, it may be a hard sell, but it can't hurt to try. It beats draining your finances and filing for bankruptcy because you can't cover the costs. So many small business owners get in over their heads with big corporations not paying within their time frame. And they know that they have the power to do so because if it ends up in court, it will be a long, expensive, and drawn-out legal battle that most small business owners can't afford.

Getting back to Mitchell's acquisitions, let's start with the painting company. Mitch was connected with a guy who owns a "big" painting company. We will call Top Dog Painting. Eric was the owner. His company is contracted with all of the Waremarts. Waremart is a large national corporate chain that is massive in size and in business. To be the contracted painter with a Waremart means that you have a consistent stream of work lined up at all times, but you have to have the funds set up to support the upfront costs as well. So he and his crew travel around from state to state to paint each Waremart.

Needless to say they had plenty of work to do, but they didn't have the funds to front the initial costs. They had to cover the cost of travel and hotel rooms for their team. They had to purchase painting supplies up front. That adds up very quickly. Think about it, painting supplies sounds like not that big of a deal, but in reality it gets quite expensive. Primer, paint, brushes, sprayers, rollers, tape, tarps, and equipment rental for lifts, and so on. The average cost to paint a room is $2.00 to $6.00 per square foot. The average size of a Waremart is 185,000 sq ft. You do the math. That's a lot of money that you have to have access to in order to be able to handle the job. On top of that, the contract read that within 30 days of the job being complete is when they would get paid. There are two problems here. Eric couldn't afford the upfront cost and even if he could afford it, Waremart never paid on time. Even though it opened Waremart up to a potential lawsuit, they just didn't care and they did not pay on time. But realistically Eric couldn't afford to have a legal battle with a big corporation. Most small business owners do not have such resources. But large corporations such as Waremarts do. In some cases, large corporations do not care about the little guy enough to make it right with them. In other cases, they may have their own financial issues going on. Point is, you have to always be prepared to handle everything that comes along with getting the job.

So Eric is introduced to Mitchell through a mutual friend. Mitchell has an entrepreneurial mind set, a generous spirit, and a business sense. So he sets up a deal with Eric where he loans Eric the necessary funds to cover his company's overhead and most importantly pays his employees. If you don't pay your employees in a timely fashion, guess what's going to happen, they are going to leave. Mitchell then formally addresses the Waremart as Eric's attorney as an attempt to retrieve the payment for a job that has been completed for well beyond the scope of the contract.

This goes on and on and continuously drags out for a ridiculous amount of time. But at least his employees were paid and his supplies and equipment charges were taken care of. Mitchell has lent Eric's company so much money and has put so many billable hours into getting Waremart to pay their debt that he was deep in. Eric now is indebted to Mitchell. They decide to resolve this payment by Mitch acquiring the company, the good, the bad, and the ugly.

Now Mitch is the owner of Top Dog Painting and he is employing Eric to manage the company for him. This way Mitch can focus on the back end and work on new contracts and negotiations. Eric was the manager, with a secure income versus the owner who doesn't take a pay until the employees are paid. There was enough work available to keep the employees busy, until there wasn't. The work being done at the Waremarts were not being done correctly. Eric was supposed to be on top of this. His job was to oversee the work being done as well as recruit new jobs. He was not handling this position.

The struggles on the business side got worse, because now the Waremarts refused to pay because the jobs were incomplete. Mitch had to use his personal finances to cover the overhead. Now Mitchell became frustrated with Eric and his disregard for the company and the work they put out. Their relationship became strained. The other employees also noticed a shift in how the company was being run. Little by little they left the company.

Soon after, Eric leaves Top Dog Painting and starts his own painting company, totally screwing Mitch over. Eric had been managing projects and employees and now Mitch had no one able to do so. Mitch was left with Top Dog Painting, no management and almost $250,000 worth of debt on jobs that Eric was supposed to have completed. Eric also borrowed a total of $75,000 in personal loans from Mitch. And guess what happened with that, crickets. Eric stops responding to Mitch and essentially falls off the face. Not cool dude!

On top of not having a noncompete agreement, Mitch never gave Eric a promissory note on the personal loan that he gave him. He treated their transactions as that of a friendship and not a business deal. Eric just moved on and didn't bat an eye at how he left Mitch with all of his debt and headaches. Even after how Mitchell helped him out. He left Mitch with a financial nightmare, no employees, tarnished the company's reputation, and continued on with his new company.

Questions

1. What could Mitch have done to avoid potential losses?

   _____

   _____

   _____

2. If you had a business skill set, would you help your friends out securing it with a verbal agreement? Why/Why not?

   _____

   _____

   _____

3. What type of document(s) could have prevented drama in this situation? Explain.

   _____

   _____

   _____

4. Why could someone who acts like a big Mahoff be targeted by scam artists?

   _____

   _____

   _____

Journal

What did you take from this chapter?

_____

_____

_____

_____

_____

CHAPTER 13

Kingpin

Figure 13 Directing your business

Photo: vitapix/iStock by Getty Images

On the streets, the word Kingpin refers to "The BOSS." Typically, it has a bit of a negative connotation since its usual reference is associated with persons engaged in illegal activity. Most people hear that word and think of the drug lord or the mob boss. A Kingpin and a Mahoff are two different stigmas as well. On the streets the Kingpin will always outweigh the Mahoff. The Mahoff acts in a way that they themselves are noticed. The Kingpin just handles their stuff, purposely noticed or completely unnoticed. Regardless, a Kingpin handles business, wherever. Who am I to define the difference between them? First off, I am a lover of a Bronx Tale and Goodfellas. Secondly, I spent a large part of my childhood living next to a bar that was owned by a legit Kingpin and had quite a few Mahoffs who hung out in there. The Kingpin ended up in prison and the Mahoffs continued to be Mahoffy, until they weren't anymore.

If you were looking at someone's social media platform, you're most likely not going to see Kingpin under their job title. The designation comes in many other forms. Let's discuss the boss's title in a legitimate business setting.

Titles such as manager, president, director, owner, and chief of a recognized identification (CEO, CFO, etc.) are some of the titles that represent authority in an organization. With authority comes power and with power comes responsibility. The boss is a recognized authority designation. The Kingpin kind of Boss leads with fist and fear. Is that the kind of boss that you want to be? This all ties right into the chapter on leadership. Often the boss is stressed out because they have a lot of responsibility on their plate. Stress leads to irritability and anger, which leads to a tense work environment.

This is where delegation comes into play. Assigning different responsibilities to different employees and assigning a manager or managers helps to free up your time so that you can work on running the business. It will help to take some of the pressure off of you. It may allow the boss to have some free personal time.

As a manager, it becomes your responsibility to take on everything that comes with having employees, especially directing them on how to successfully take part in running the business successfully. The starting point is being an excellent role model. A good figurehead shows grace and composure during good times and in bad. Are you able to stay composed during a stressful time at work? Are you able to leave your personal life at the door and not bring your outside problems into work? You need to be. This is especially if you expect your team to show a high level of composure and professionalism.

Whatever the title, a chief has to demonstrate and communicate confidence. To demonstrate a confident decision-making attitude reassures your team that they are going in the right direction. This in turn will benefit the team and the company. But there is a difference between being confident and being full of themselves, those in a superior position who are overly confident or full of themselves can be a turn-off to employees. Arrogance is not appealing. You are not sending a message from which you will get a positive return. A top dog that just barks orders at people in a demanding tone creates a tense and hostile environment. You don't have to act like a Kingpin to gain the respect of those around you.

A manager should be proud yet humble about their position. Even if you are the most amazing person for the job, the recipient of every award known to man, be humble about it. People will notice how great you are, you do not need to flaunt it.

Encourage Feedback

Encourage feedback. No one person knows it all. Things are constantly changing. Be open-minded to suggestions and changes and allow your team to be heard. It's not just about just listening to them; make sure that they understand that you are actually absorbing what they are saying.

If you're having a one-on-one meeting, be sure to repeat back what is being said to you. This will let them know that you are hearing what they are telling you and processing what they are saying. Even if it's something that you may not agree with, let them know that their ideas and concerns are appreciated.

Excellent commanders come to surface under pressure. There are countless issues that can come to surface being an employer or a manager. It's important to remember that how you deal with each situation is being monitored by your team. Take a breath before you speak or act and handle a stressful situation with grace and tact.

Be sure to take the time to get to know your team. In this day and age, the phrase "My way or the highway" doesn't really fly anymore. Employees know they have options. People value themselves and the idea of living their best lives more than they value their jobs. They have the advantage of social media job sites that highlight all the options that they have to choose from.

Studies show that in the time frame around 2020 the average length of time that an employee spends with a company is approximately four years, and that's on the high end. Back in the day, people spent lifetime careers with the same company. Jobs lasted for 15 to 40 years. People then were very grateful for their jobs and there wasn't a lot of thought about better opportunities for them. It was more about gratitude for what they had. But again this was before social media and even before the Internet. There was limited exposure as to what the world had to offer. Times have changed. Big time.

In the modern day, workplace things have shifted in a very different direction. People these days usually start out excited and grateful to get a new job. But before long they quickly start to think about what's next.

What's better? What's more exciting? What's going to pay me more? What job can I do less work and make more money? Is the grass always greener on the other side? Sometimes it is, but sometimes it's simply greener where you water it.

Employees want to know what you are going to offer them. They also want to feel accomplished. They want to make a difference in the success of a project, or the overall performance of a company. They want to know that they are appreciated. As a team leader, you need to help fulfill that need. Positive reinforcements and compliments go such a long way.

Recognizing Performance

When an employee lands the job they desperately wanted they are so excited and motivated. They give it their all. After a while, they put in some time to their position and start to see themselves as valuable in your company, and that's where something can shift in their performance.

There can be a mindset trigger in which they begin to overvalue themselves. Typically, you can see it happening. Their behavior starts to change. You may see them get less motivated. You may see their energy decrease or their appearance change. They may start to show up late or just on time versus the early person they used to be. You always be on the lookout and pay attention to changes such as these.

Employee's mindset changes can be obvious or they can be low-key and subtle. More obvious signs that an employee is unhappy show themselves in the way of their attitude. A decrease in energy becomes obvious. They may become quieter than usual. They may not have the same "team player" attitude that they previously had. Their work can go from "above and beyond" to "doing what they have to do." Physical changes such as wardrobe, hair, and makeup are other signs. When someone who may typically be very put together shows a lack of caring in their physical appearance, that is a tell-tale sign that something is off.

That's when it is your time to make a boss decision. You can have a one-on-one meeting with them and do a check in. That's if you want to have a chance of keeping them around for a while longer. Sit them down, have an emotionally intelligent conversation and see what's going on with them. Really tap in to your own emotional intelligence and have a professional yet caring conversation with them. Show them empathy and understanding. Based on feedback that they give you, together you both can make a plan on how to reset their goals and motivate them again. Once that is complete, the ball is in their court.

The second option is to simply let them drift away and wait for them to leave. Sometimes it's just their time to move on. It doesn't have to be a bad thing. But it's nice when an employee leaves in a civil manner and in generally good terms.

Then there is the self-destruct mode. They will self-destruct if they feel stuck. This creates a toxic environment. Try to get ahead of that. Have that one-on-one and let them know that it's OK to move on. It will help keep the environment drama free.

Understanding Motives

I've seen it all. Realistically there are some people who I have been really disappointed to see leave, but they had reasons that I as an employer couldn't compete with. So as unfortunate that it was to see them go, I was genuinely happy for them to have an opportunity that was better for their life in the moment. The beauty of that is that employees like this will always have an option to come back.

There were some employees who left and it was like a giant weight being lifted from my shoulders. They created a toxic environment bashing the business, bashing the leadership, coaching other employees to leave the company, and brainwashing clients to leave with them so the clients would not come back to the business after this. They may want to destroy the reputation of a leader as well as their business just so they can benefit from that destruction. You could be the best boss around, but if someone wants what you have, if they are jealous, if they don't like you, or if they just want to take you down, they can and will create a story of lies and twisted occurrences to make themselves look like a victim. This is all a ploy to destroy. They can file false lawsuits and make claims that are outright lies.

Unfortunately, these people are hard to detect. They are usually the wolves in sheep's clothing. This is why leading with emotional intelligence is very important as well as doing periodic check-ins. Get a read on your team. Try to avoid being the Kingpin that gets taken out by one of your own. Your most trusted side kick may darn well have a hit out on you and you don't even know it.

Why would your employee want to destroy your business? The most popular reason is because they have an agenda. They either plan to starting their own business or join another business that may be competitive to yours. Obviously, they don't want to look bad. So they paint a picture of this horrible company that they had to escape from. They start their own business and recruit as many clients of yours that they can. For these types of employees there is no changing direction. They have an agenda. **So pay attention, get ahead of them, and get them out before it's too late.**

Some people are sensitive and have to be treated accordingly. Some people respond better to direct orders. Learning what approach each team member responds best to is truly important. The world is full of sensitive people these days. Sometimes it simply comes down to not being that person's cup of tea. Meaning they simply do not like you. Nothing you can say or do will change that.

As I mentioned already, leading with fear is only going to get you so far. Leading with mutual respect is hands down the way to go and grow! If you are already not someone's cup of tea and you dictate with fear, it can end poorly for everyone involved. Put this phrase in your arsenal, if it's not already there. "It's not what you say, it's how you say it." Say it again. "It's not what you say, it's how you say it." And one more time, "It's not what you say, it's how you say it." This line isn't mine to claim. But it is one of the most important things you can use in life. This doesn't just go for in your workplace: it is applicable for all relationships. Always be mindful of your tone and keep it professional.

This all ties into the importance of how having positive relationships with people will help to build a good network. Having a good network is always good for business as well as in life. If you put out positivity you will get it in return.

One of my other favorite phrases is: "You can catch more flies with honey than you do with vinegar." Now I'm not sure who came up with this phrase. Who is trying to catch flies anyway? But the meaning behind is what's appealing. Sweetness is more appealing than bitterness, even to a fly.

Setting Expectations

Now, in no way am I suggesting that you have to coddle your employees. You can be firm. Just be sure to speak in a tone that is not degrading. Speaking to people in a kind tone will be received well. It will be significantly more appreciated than being talked down to. People do not respond well to those who speak to them in a degrading way. If that is you, then that is something that you have to work on. If you are not a respected leader then it will eventually catch up with you.

There is another side to this though. If someone came from a place where aggression or anger was a tone that they are used to, they may mistake your kindness for weakness. Some people may respond well to an aggressive tone. Aggressive, not degrading; no one will respond well to degrading. I cannot stress that enough.

I have heard many stories of bosses who were extremely difficult to work for. They screamed at their employees and literally had tantrums. They threw objects across the room. They were degrading and abusive. And in this day and age, that type of behavior will catch up to you, and not in a good way. So be sure to mind your manners.

You have to be sure that there are proper warnings and communicated consequences established with all employees. For the employees who may not be receptive to a gentler approach in the workplace, needs to know that you will not take any nonsense either. That is where the employee handbook comes into play.

The employee handbook will establish rules, regulations, and protocols of your business. Having guidelines written down is crucial to keeping every one of your employees on the same page. The expectations are set so it takes the guess work out of what is expected from the team. The reality is that you never know what personality you will be employing. This is why it is helpful to understand your employees and learn what approach to take with each individual.

Questions

1. Think about a boss that you know. Name a positive quality that they have.

_____

_____

_____

2. Why is this quality so appealing to you?

_____

_____

_____

3. Think of a management example that you experienced that was not appealing. Why?

_____

_____

_____

4. What is something that you will do to be a good boss?

_____

_____

_____

Journal

What did you take from this chapter?

_____

_____

_____

_____

_____

CHAPTER 14

Promoting Your Business

Figure 14 *Design, logo, brand, trust, marketing, advertising, loyalty, and quality*

Photo: EtiAmmos/iStock by Getty Images

The success of your business is based on a lot of factors. But first it starts out with finding the right name. You want to make sure that you have a name that is clearly read, easily spelled, and easy to pronounce. It should sound good when saying it out loud and roll easily off the tongue. This is your brand. This is how you want the world to view you.

After you take the time to brainstorm your business name, have a little fun with it. Write it down, say it out loud, and share it with some of your closest friends and family members. Get some feedback but remember that it ultimately comes down to you and what you are naming your business, so make sure that you are good with the name that you finally chose.

You will need to do a business name search. Doing a thorough web search you will likely find the same name that is already being used by another business owner. Regardless, if you do or do not find your business twin name out there, you will want to do a proper search to make sure there are no trademarks attached to the business name. You can do a search at USPTO.gov to find out if it already exists or it's available for you to trademark. You can also hire a lawyer to take care of it.

You should also scope out a business search through your Secretary of State's records. If the name that you chose is too similar to a name in their records, you may not get approved for the name to be registered. A corporate attorney is highly recommended to have during the start-up process. They will have access to do any legal search that is necessary as well as provide guidance through the start-up process. Be prepared to pay $300 to $500 per hour for their expertise. Consider it a well-spent cost of doing business.

Now that you have named your business, it's time to go to the next step. This part can be quite fun but it can also be creatively overwhelming.

Your logo concept. Logo design is an important part of your brand recognition. Do you want your design to be sleek, bubbly, bold, naturalist, feminine, or masculine? You get the point. It's your vibe that you want to come across to your audience through your logo. Remember **YOUR VIBE ATTRACTS YOUR TRIBE.** This is really going to play into your target audience. The steps you are going to take to attract your customers are key. You can hire a logo designer or a graphic designer to assist in the final design. But you should start the process having a clear vision of what your goal is. The designer can help customize the artwork to your vision.

Personally speaking, I had an inspired vision of my current business logo. I decided to continue to use my maiden name for my business. I was involved in my family business and I feel that there is something special about that. I thought about rebranding and starting new, but my family history is something that I hold close to my heart. It's where I am rooted. We are a large family filled with generations of salon owners, barbers, and stylists. I love that about us. Our family history is often a topic. As well as is our family tree. A tree and branches was a conversation between all of the family in the industry at one point when we were going to brand our businesses together. It was an exciting time for my family of hair peeps and salon owners. We even created a piolet for a reality show. It didn't quite work out because we didn't want to throw brushes at each other on camera, but it was a fun experience. I really was inspired by the idea of a family tree. But instead of a tree, I thought more along the lines of roots. Roots and hair and scissors, it just goes together. So I sketched out a logo drawing. I'm far from an artist but the concept was there. It was then given to a tattoo artist who was able to transform my raw sketch into a cool artistic design. Last it went to a graphic designer for finalization. And although the name of my business is just my last name, the logo tells a story.

Brand Strategy

Your brand is the overall perception that the public thinks of about your business. Your main goal in brand building is to gain the attention of any possible consumers, then capture them and hold their attention in a positive light.

Branding is not something that happens overnight. It takes time to build a brand. It takes consistency and most importantly, it takes work. Just like everything involved in business building, you have to put in the work. I can't stress this enough! You have to do the work!

Brand strategy will allow you to figure out a plan to convey your purpose. You can map out different ideas as to how to gain your audience's attention. This is where you want to take the time to create your mission and tell your story. This is your opportunity to demonstrate what sets you apart from your competitors? Your passion and your purpose are unique and building your brand strategy around this is critical. This applies in the start-up phase as well as down the line with rebranding missions.

Now that you have created the **ATTENTION** phase of your brand strategy let's gain our audience's trust. Make them trust you! Give them every reason to believe that you are going to deliver on your promises. Once they give you a shot and you deliver on your promises you will gain their **TRUST**. They trust you and they want to support you, so they come back and again you deliver on your promises and provide an excellent experience for your customer. That's where something special happens. That trust turns into a special relationship and **LOYALTY** is built. Gaining the trust of your customers is hard enough to do, but gaining their loyalty is something special and you don't want to take that for granted.

You have to appreciate and value your loyal customers by expressing your appreciation to them. Guess what will happen, they will **ADVOCATE** for your business. They will support and refer new customers to your business because you have given them every reason to want to do so.

Fun fact: Studies show that a high percentage of people will purchase from a company based on their brand values and impact. Did you hear that? Make an impressionable impact and make your brand memorable.

Definitely remember when you're planning your branding strategy, how important all these things are, and plan accordingly. Your brand should be promoted consistently across all platforms. You will want to promote your brand with your logo at any given opportunity.

Brand Marketing

Brand marketing is the opportunity for a business to bring awareness to the services and/or products they provide by telling your audience about it through strategic communication. Some communications come free and some require payment. Such communications consist of social media platforms, website experience, e-mail marketing campaigns, magazines, radio, and TV.

There are also many other forms of paid advertising. For example, sponsorships are a large part of paid advertising. Anywhere from little league sports to big charity auctions, sponsorships provide an opportunity to get in front of different people.

As important as it is to capture your audience with your business brand, your personal brand should be worked into your brand marketing plan. People connect with people. So to allow a bit of yourself to come through and this will remind people that they are not just supporting a "business," they are supporting a person(s). It becomes a little more personal for the consumer and they appreciate that.

You should also allow your audience to have a peek behind the curtain. If your employees are comfortable with being highlighted, then definitely do so. Allow your customers to see the people behind the scenes who make the company flow and provide them with a great experience. Show them who they are supporting. It's strategic marketing, but it is also genuine. It goes a long way.

Here is a marketing plan worksheet for you to develop your marketing strategy. Use this to guide you to think about how you want to stimulate your business.

Marketing Plan Worksheet

- **Name of business**

_____

- **Products and services**

_____

_____

_____

- **Target market**
  List the audience who will use these products and services by writing the description of the individuals or companies. Age/Gender/Income

_____

_____

_____

- **Frequency of consumer**
  List how often customers will potentially utilize your products or services.

_____

_____

_____

- **Benefits**
  List the benefits of products and services that are offered to your consumer.

_____

_____

_____

- **Competition**
  List the direct competitors that your business will have.

  _____

  _____

  _____

- **Stand out**
  List what sets you apart from your competitors. Why should they choose your business?

  _____

  _____

  _____

- **Seek and find**
  List ways on how you plan on finding customers through paid marketing.

  _____

  _____

  _____

- **Free marketing options**

  _____

  _____

  _____

- **Marketing budget**
  List how much money you set aside for marketing overall.

  _____

- **Distribution of funds**
  List how you will distribute the funds to each marketing method listed previously.

  _____

  _____

  _____

Now that you have your brand strategy covered it's time to take all of this information and apply it to your website design. You want to convey the three most important things in your website design.

- **WHAT** products or services do you offer?

  _____

  _____

  _____

- **HOW** are you set apart from your competitors?

  _____

  _____

  _____

- **Why** should customers/clients come to you?

  _____

  _____

  _____

This is the perfect opportunity to share your passion with your audience.

You may be ready to design your own website or you can use a web design company.

There are many companies out there that are built to help you design your own website. Sites such as GoDaddy, Wix, Squarespace, and Weebly are a few reputable website builders. WordPress is an extremely popular platform as far as content management goes. Your host and domain name are done separately.

After you have determined the purpose of your website there are a few steps that you will need to take.

- **Decide your domain name**

  Do a proper search to make sure the name you chose is available. The perfect domain name will identify your website so make sure that is clear and memorable. In most cases the domain name reflects the brand name.

- **Pick your template**

  Your template provides the vibe of your business, so this is the opportunity for you to paint the canvas for your audience's interpretation.

- **Build your pages**

  Determine what you would like to relate to your audience page by page. You can offer page(s) of your products and services, pricing, and hours. Include a page about your team and a page telling your business's story. It's really up to you what information you want on your pages.

- **Set up your payment system**

  Link your point of sale, credit card processing, Pay Pal, Apple Pay, Zelle, Venmo, or any other future accounts used to collect payment.

- **Set up online booking**

  If you are service-based business you will want to create an option for people to schedule online.

- **Link your social media pages**

  Constantly changing photos on your website can be time consuming. If you link your social media pages this will allow your posts and pictures to filter through your website.

- **Test and publish your website**

  Be sure to preview your website before you go live.
  > Check all spelling and grammar.
  > Make sure all of the buttons are functioning.
  > Inspect the visual aspect.
  > Check it out on a desktop and mobile.
  > Make sure you love it!

Now all of this same information will apply if you decide to go with a web design company. The difference is that they will guide you through the process and handle all of the work. You will still need to provide them with the same general information to apply to your website. There are tons of web design companies. A quick Google search will help you find one that is right for you. Always take a moment to read reviews and check out their sample pages.

OK, now you have your website mapped out. Your social media is actively flowing through your site. Make sure your social media is consistent with your brand. Social media is one of the most effective tools to market your brand! It allows you to engage with your audience regularly and show them what your business is about.

Social media will allow you to gain the **attention** of followers who can potentially ...

transform to customers. At that point you gain their **trust** by ...

providing them with an excellent experience with your business.

This in turn gains your business ...

loyal *customers that will* **advocate** *for your biz!*

And this is all free and placed directly in front of their faces at the touch of their phone!

You can boost your social media posts by paying for it. You have the ability to specifically choose your audience. It allows you to pick out a radius meaning a specific distance of a location. You can choose by gender or by age. So if you wanted to do a post on a specific product for an established gentleman, you can pay specifically for only men of a certain age to get the post. It's a great way to spend your marketing dollars.

Don't give up on the good old business card though. There are still times when a business card exchange comes into play. There are plenty of networking events that may allow the opportunity to exchange your card with a potential client. Even if it's not a designated networking event, something as simple as meeting someone out at a bar or restaurant and chatting about what you do for a living could be the perfect opportunity to exchange your card. Don't rule these opportunities out because guess what ... not everyone uses social media believe it or not! Sometimes it just calls for a card exchange versus an Instagram handle exchange.

Now you have it, ladies and gents! You are able to plan out your marketing strategy, design your website, and start the adventure of building your business.

Questions

1. Is marketing your business yourself something that is appealing to you? Why or why not?

_____

_____

_____

2. What tools would you be most inclined to use in marketing your business?

_____

_____

_____

3. Would you be comfortable putting yourself out there personally in order to allow people to know the person behind the business? Why or why not?

_____

_____

_____

Journal

What did you take from this chapter?

_____

_____

_____

_____

_____

CHAPTER 15

It's Not What You Know...

Figure 15 It's who you know

Photo: Zinkevych/iStock by Getty Images

Mitch acquired a landscaping company. Think of it as a similar situation that happened between Mitch and Eric. This company has big contracts. The company owner struggles to collect payments. The company and the company's owner is drowning in debt. Owner comes to Mitch with an opportunity, which translated into "he needs help." Mitch, the optimistic entrepreneur that he is, decided to get involved with the opportunity that he is presented with.

Earthy Landscaping Company has been around for years. Owned and operated by a father/son dynamic duo, this company has a reputation known for quality work and excellent service. They have contracts with the city for certain projects. They also contract with large property developers, private schools, and corporate land maintenance.

In the winter they have some snow removal contracts in place. One of these contracts is actually subcontracted out through the company that was awarded the general contract through the city. So they have to wait for the snow to fall to do the work. If and when the snow falls, they go to the assigned job site. They are required to take before and after pictures to submit with their invoice as proof of completion. They are paid according to the amount of snow fall that is reported by the national weather service in a specific area.

After the invoices are submitted to the middle man company, the company then submits the same information to the city. The city has 30 days to pay for each invoice submitted. Then the middleman has 10 days to pay after they receive payment. So Earthy Landscape Company is prepared for a 40-day hold on receiving payment. They still have to make their payroll and pay everyone who worked 30-hour shifts during the snowstorms. They had to cover the cost of the salt upfront. They had to purchase more equipment because some of the snowblowers weren't working, shovels and ice scrapers were breaking due to how heavy the snow and ice was. They had to have access to funds to cover the entire cost without payment for 40 days.

Six months later, here we are in July. The landscaping company has still not been paid for the work they did back in December. Crazy right?

In the meantime, Mitch's wife is seeing changes in Mitch. He's irritable and not sleeping. He is stressed out beyond words. She asked him what's going on. He breaks down the scenario and is up front about the situation. Because of these back payments he had to use their personal money to pay the employees for their labor and it trickled down six months and effected budgets for other projects.

Mitch's wife reached out to a friend of hers who works for the city, asking if she can look into this. Did the middleman get paid and is stalling on paying Earthy for their work? The middleman company is saying that the city never paid them therefore they cannot pay Earthy Landscaping. Did the city never actually pay them? What is actually going on here?

Interestingly enough, soon after things get looked into from authority on the inside, they finally got paid. They could have dug a little deeper to see if it were a breach of contract with the middleman, but getting involved in a legal battle isn't always worth the time, energy, and money.

Sometimes it's not what you know, it's who you know that gets you somewhere. Actually that is most of the time. OK, so we have that summed up.

Now here we are back to the same number one issue across the board ... collecting payment. Believe it or not, when in business most people/companies do not start off with an intention on purposely screwing other people or companies over. Typically, a business agreement starts out with good intentions. But I'm going to take it back to basics and remind you that bad stuff happens. People get in over their head and poor decision making happens.

Let's start with the property developers. You see the same names all over these days on new construction sites. These are the companies that have put a working system into play. This means that they have figured out a process to access capital.

Typically it works as follows: Builder goes to bank for a construction loan. The bank assesses the plans and if the plans look promising to the bank then you are approved. But hold your horses Mr. Builder; you have to come up with some cash-ola on your own in order to get started because the bank doesn't distribute the funds until you are at a certain level of completion. Mr. Builder comes up with the capital. Like I said before it's not until jobs are completed, phase by phase, that the bank issues you the money. They come out to inspect the work that has been done and once the bank inspector sees that everything is going according to plan, they give the thumbs up and release the funds.

These funds apply to all aspects of the job, including the landscape architecture. That ranges from the landscape of each property to the trees lining the streets and greenery in common areas. The builder has a construction loan with the bank. He also has a contract with the landscaping company.

The landscaping company has to come out and do the work. They have to come out of pocket for all labor costs, materials, plants, trees, and so on. They have to wait for the builder to pay them. The builder is waiting for the bank to come out and inspect the work that was done. Once that is done they have to wait for the bank to release the funds. It's exhausting and everyone is stressed out completely. This often leads to a strain on the relationships of contractors and subcontractors, often ending with bad blood over payment issues.

But if they all financially planned appropriately this should be survivable, and not only does everyone eventually get paid, they all actually make a profit instead of constantly treading water. And if they didn't financially plan accordingly, and they don't have a line of credit to access or a nest egg built up and if something goes wrong during the project, then they are not in good shape and can lead to companies filing for bankruptcy. The banks protocols rule these situations and the business owners are left scrambling. Just know what you're getting into before getting into it. Don't let the big payout number entice you and mislead you thinking that you have this easy contract of doing the work and getting paid the big bucks. Be prepared for delays of payment and bumps in the road and be sure to factor what you have to cover in the interim.

Questions

1. What are some ways to access funds for cash flow?

   _____

   _____

   _____

2. What are some ways to collect payment from big corporations that are late on their payments?

   _____

   _____

   _____

3. Do you think it is worth having consistent work with companies that pay well but that are consistently late on their payments? Why/ Why not?

   _____

   _____

   _____

4. What are some ways you can strategize and negotiate with companies to try to plan for a successful business relationship?

   _____

   _____

   _____

Journal

What did you take from this chapter?

_____

_____

_____

_____

_____

CHAPTER 16

Underdog

Figure 16 Rising to the top

Photo: IPGGutenbergUKLtd/iStock by Getty Images

Everybody loves an underdog. If you don't know about the underdog, it is the team that always struggles and then comes out of nowhere for the win. The person who goes from rags to riches is an everyday hero. It's the American Dream, it's actually everyone's dream. But there's something that happens when you get there, way up high. It becomes a challenge to try to stay there.

It's hard enough to get there in the land of success. Then you have to factor all of the underlying issues behind it. People try to tear you down. Look at teams such as the New England Patriots and the New York Yankees in the 2000s. Unless you're a fan, you are cheering against them just because they always win. For some reason, people don't like when teams always win. Just like people do not like people who always win, even when they put in the work. Unfortunately, there are a lot more haters out there than we would like to think.

Trina's Story

Some people just can never seem to catch a break. Every time there is an opportunity to get ahead, something happens to set them back. Some people are just dealt a bad hand from the start. These types of people and situations are examples of the underdogs. Who doesn't love a great story of a person who has experienced adversity in their youth and manages to have happiness and success later on in life?

Trina and her siblings were raised by a single mother after their parents divorced at a young age. Their other sibling chose to leave their mother and went to live with her father. At mom's house there were rules and chores; at dad's house she had complete freedom. She abandoned her mother and her siblings for many years, because she moved and never looked back. She refused to even speak to her mother for years. Their mother was diagnosed with cancer. She fought this cancer for years.

The community pulled together to try to help this struggling family. They delivered meals and helped pitch in to take care of the kids and the property. The kids ranged in ages from 1 year old to 12 years old. And in the last year of her life her eldest daughter, who was now 20 years old, showed up. This was just in time to allow herself to have peace, when her mother was on her death bed. Trina's mother raised her kids to the best of her ability. Eventually the cancer won and their sick mother passed away. All of the kids ended up living with their father sharing a tiny studio apartment.

Throughout their childhood people always tried to help out. They were now being raised by a struggling single father. He had his own struggles. He struggled with addiction and with mental health issues. He eventually was able to seek help in a mental health facility. These kids were the underdogs by circumstance, even though it didn't feel that way.

Trina always seemed to have a hard time when it came to her education. She had a learning disability and struggled her way through school. As much as she would have loved to go to college, her father was convinced that college wasn't for her. So he asked her to join him to work at his hardware store.

Fred, Trina's father, opened the store years before Trina was even born. Fred had five other kids who grew up, went to college, and followed their own dreams in different careers. They were good students in school and didn't have the same struggles that Trina did, learning.

Change of Ownership

Trina worked with her father for over 20 years. As Trina took control of running the business, she was able to expand it and she opened other locations on her own and really built up the company. Trina developed a little corner hardware store into a successful company with multiple locations. In the meantime, none of his other kids wanted any parts of the business. They all had their own lives and were successful in their professions. They came to the store when they needed something and that was their only interaction with the business.

To no one's surprise, once Fred was in his 70s he sold the business to his daughter. He started to slow down and didn't want to deal with all of the aggravation that comes with running a business.

A few years after they did the legal business transfer, he sold the building to Trina as well. They set a payment plan out that Fred had all of his debt gone and had additional income coming in every month. He was never in the financial position to set him up with a retirement savings. So this payment structure gave him a steady stream of cash flow. It wasn't tons but it was more than he could have ever had. It worked out great for Fred and he really appreciated all of the sacrifice and hard work that his daughter did for him to be debt free and put money in his bank. It also worked out nicely for Trina, all of the years of hard work and dedication to her father's business was now a bonus to her.

A few years later Fred was diagnosed with the big C. As he started his cancer treatment plan, Fred's other kids suddenly took an interest in the business. They saw their elderly father was in bad health and wanted to make sure that his financial affairs were lined up. Fred passed away and they discovered that he didn't have any money to be left for them, because he lived his life spending and giving and not saving. They became angry because they saw Trina was now the owner of a seemingly successful business. This was a business that none of them ever had a part of, yet they felt entitled to it. They tried to sue Trina for the value of the business. Trina offered them the business to own and operate themselves. All they had to do was reimburse her the money that she had paid her father for it a few years ago. They didn't want the business or the work that comes along with running it, they just wanted money that they felt entitled to.

They didn't care that this business expansion was funded by her alone and that their father ultimately had no capital or involved in the expansion. They also didn't care that she purchased the building years prior, and they didn't have an inheritance because the money he received paid off his debt. It was no secret. They were kept in the loop and offered the opportunity to help him out of his debt. They didn't want to help him, yet they felt entitled to a business and building that they had no parts of both legally or ethically, and that's the bottom line.

They continuously harassed and threatened her. They spread vicious lies and circulated rumors about her tricking her father into signing the business and building over to her. It caused customers to stop coming into Trina's business. Friends and neighbors chimed in on the gossip and helped to spread a story that was untrue. It damaged Trina's reputation in a community that she was a part of for so long. So, Trina gave in. She took out a loan and gave each of them a significant amount of money. They had no right to a business that wasn't theirs, but Trina felt that the continuous fighting wasn't worth the heartache. She struggled to pay the loan back because she already had a loan that she took out to pay her dad for everything years ago. She continued for a while until she couldn't afford to operate the business. Between multiple loans, rent, payroll, and basic operating costs, she just couldn't afford it. Besides, she had her own living expenses and children to take care of. This year, she closed her business, laid her father to rest, and never spoke to her siblings again. She took on more debt than her business could support just to make everyone happy. But they all got a nice payout so they didn't care that she was left to close her business and without a job.

Point of the story is everybody loves an underdog. Everyone roots for the people who are struggling. They love to see them rise and they love to see them fall.

Money makes people do crazy things. Make sure you have every business transaction in a signed agreement regarding your business arrangement, even when dealing with family members. Trina would have had to come up with a significant amount of money in order to keep her business. The undocumented financial transactions that happened previously between this father/daughter duo caused a lot of confusion among who those who didn't know the full situation and had an agenda.

The long and short of this story is to make sure every transaction between business partners and associates is documented in full. And always watch your back because when you rise to the top of your game, the haters are going to want you to lose, and unfortunately some will stop at nothing to see you fall.

Questions

1. Name a famous underdog who was on top and then fell? What happened to them?

   _____

   _____

   _____

2. Would you make an unwarranted payout for peace of mind, even if the person(s) on the receiving end weren't entitled to it?

   _____

   _____

   _____

3. What are your goals at this moment?

   _____

   _____

   _____

4. What steps are you currently taking to fulfill your goals? Who is supporting you and helping to reach them?

   _____

   _____

   _____

Journal

What did you take from this chapter?

_____

_____

_____

_____

_____

CHAPTER 17

The Gamble

Figure 17 Securing your finances

Photo: Image Source/iStock by Getty Images

A lot of kids in the city grew up pitching pennies or pitching quarters. Have you heard of that? As a kid we would collect any change we could. On the weekends we would meet up to pitch pennies, or quarters or nickels or dimes, whatever we could get our hands on. The point of the game was to pitch your coin from behind a designated line. The line was either a score in the sidewalk or made with a few pebbles that we found.

We would try to get the coin closest to the wall without hitting the wall. The person who had the closest coin got to keep all the change. There was a gamble involved, but in the world of making money there usually is. It all comes down to the same thing, you make money or you lose money. But remember that you always have the option not to play. You can just work and save and instead of gambling and taking financial risk, you can put all of those coins in your piggy bank.

We just read about Trina and her father, Fred. Fred worked hard his whole life as a small business owner. He had a nice income flowing in but he could never seem to get ahead. Like a lot of folks, he spent most of his younger years treading water financially. Unfortunately, by the time he was into his retirement age he was financially underwater. Now, if Fred sat down with a financial advisor early on he may have been able to establish some discipline in his spending and saving habits and set himself up for his financial future. Back in the day, the world of financial advisors wasn't quite a thing. Actually, the first graduating class of the College of Financial Planning happened in 1973. Between then and 1982 there was a double recession in our country. It wasn't until the mid-1980s that financial planning became a thing. In 1987, there were only 20 colleges that offered programs for registered financial planners. In 2005, that number increased to 190 colleges offering a variety of 300 programs for registered planners. The point is, it took time to build this field's growth and bring awareness to the importance of planning for your future. Many of our parents and grandparents didn't have this opportunity or know how. The upside to being an employee for a larger corporation is that they set things up for you. Many companies provide things like a 401K and different retirement and savings plans. As a self-employed business owner, that is all on you to do for yourself. There is no handholding involved. So you must take the wheel, and drive yourself to find the right financial advisor to work with that will help you set realistic goals for your future.

Go to Thinkadvisor.com and look up the article written on December 1, 2005 by Kate McBride. It is titled, "The History of Financial Planning." It provides a thorough summary on how financial planning came to be and all of the beginning struggles that had to be worked through. By understanding the history of a specific topic or idea we are able to gain a better perspective all around.

A Financial Advisor

What exactly is a financial advisor? It is pretty self-explanatory. A financial advisor is someone who advises you on how to improve and secure your finances. They will help to map out and create strategies to increase financial wealth all while eliminating risk. The goal is to basically create a game plan to establish long-term financial wealth. It also allows the opportunity for an individual to pay down their debt if need by calculating a formulated plan.

Often the idea of having a financial advisor or a wealth manager is associated with being rich or wealthy. Do not be deterred or intimated by that. Even if you don't have a lot of money to put away, it is still a smart idea to consult with a professional and plan for your future. It will be here before you know it.

Listen, in all reality most financial advisors want the clients who have a lot of money to put up. The more money you make, it affects their income in a positive way. But there are plenty of financial advisors who help people from all walks of life. Talk to your friends and family members to see who they work with. Word of mouth is always a great resource. Then do your own homework and check out their background. It is always a good idea to read reviews, do professional background checks, and follow your gut. You are trusting this person with your personal information and your financial life.

Now, financial advisors deal with things such as stocks, mutual funds, and different types of savings options. There is a level of risk involved. Some people look at it as legal gambling when you get into the stock market. It very well may be, but that doesn't mean that you have to throw the dice. There are much safer options. All of your options will be presented and discussed during the consultation with a financial planner. Again, these are all things that you should do your homework on ahead of time and after the fact, so that you have an educated understanding of your options. Suck up all of the information that you possibly can.

In the story of Trina and Fred, Trina presented her oldest sibling the opportunity to take part in helping their father out of his debt. She was in a very good financial position at that point in her life. She was also very good at saving and had a great financial investment plan set up for herself.

She told Trina that she did not want to be involved in helping their father out of his debt. She made it very clear. Fred didn't ask Trina because he knew that she would not help him financially. He would always joke about how frugal his eldest child was saying things like "She still has her lunch money from middle school." Trina did not bother to ask the other siblings because they were in no financial position to help and often had to take or borrow money from their father to cover their own financial hardships. The fact that he would borrow or take money from Trina and give or lend money to his other kids did not help with the family dynamic.

Fred's lack of financial planning took a long-term effect on not just him, but his family and his business. Unfortunately, when he arrived at retirement age range he wasn't prepared. This ended up with him living a retirement lifestyle that he wouldn't have preferred if he had planned differently.

Questions

1. Have you ever been exposed to the concept of financial planning? If so who do you have to thank for showing you the way?

   _____

   _____

   _____

2. Have you ever gambled? If so, did you like it? Why/Why not?

   _____

   _____

   _____

3. If you have not started thinking about saving for your future, at what age do you plan on doing so?

   _____

   _____

   _____

4. Would you be willing to sacrifice a couple of fun nights out to put money into your savings for your retirement? Why/Why not?

   _____

   _____

   _____

Journal

What did you take from this chapter?

_____

_____

_____

_____

_____

CHAPTER 18

Risky Business

Figure 18 The entrepreneur

Photo: Targovcom/iStock by Getty Images

Speaking of gambling, let's talk about the entrepreneur. The entrepreneur is always an interesting type of person. Any person who has a desire to start a business or invest in a business tends to be a risk taker. The question is ... just how risky are they?

First, let's touch on the entrepreneur who is wholeheartedly invested. This person is in it to win it. They have a passion and a vested interest in their business idea. They have their business plan all laid out. They have personal funds set aside to get things going and they are ready to grind! Now as an investor, this just may be the person you want to back financially.

If you want to invest your money into something or someone, this is your person, provided that their idea and plan is idealistic, the research is complete, and there is a market for it. If they have skin in the game and they are putting in the same amount of capital or at least a fair amount of capital contribution in comparison to the other investors that becomes an incentive for them to work smarter and harder.

Next we have entrepreneurs who have big ideas. Usually those who have big ideas have amazing plans to go along with it. When they are pitching their ideas to their investors, their whole presentation is extremely exciting. They explain things in such a hyped-up way that it gives you an incredible visual. You start getting excited along with them. You can see their vision, you can almost touch it. This business plan sounds like exactly what you're looking for. The question is, are they prepared to get this idea out of their head and into reality? It's easy to have ideas, the hard part is bringing them to fruition. Let's say that as an investor you don't want to do any work. You just want to be an investor or perhaps a silent partner. And then Einstein comes along with a brilliant plan, and suddenly you start feeling his excitement and seeing his vision and want to be a part of it … you hear cha-ching! You can almost smell the money ringing in. The return on your investment looks and sounds almost too good to be true! This person is a genius! You want in immediately. This idea is amazing! Where do you sign? Awesome, right?

Wrong!

You forgot something major. What, you wonder?

Well, I'm sorry to crush your dreams but you forgot to ask one huge question. Let me tell you what that question is …

Does Einstein have skin in the game?

As I mentioned, there's something to be said for having skin in the game. The phrase "skin in the game" refers to having personal risk involved to achieve a goal, usually referring to monetary contribution. When a person is directly involved and has something to lose, they operate a little differently, a little more efficiently. Anyone can paint a good picture and tell you what you want to hear. But if they are not taking any risk themselves, then you better take a step back and reevaluate the situation.

I know, I know, in business it's a common theory to try to not use your own money. Ultimately a start-up company (person/people) wants to raise capital by using other people's money. Start-up entrepreneurs are coached into this mindset. Hey, good for them if they can find people to contribute! But do you really want to be that person? I don't recommend it.

For an entrepreneur to find investors to contribute to your company sounds like a great idea. This avoids you having to come up with the finances all by yourself. It takes the pressure off of your financial contribution. But keep in mind that the more investors and/or partners that you have, the less money you are going to make. You have that many more people to pay out. Do your research and look into taking out business loans from multiple sources and pay close attention to the interest that you are committing to pay back.

When Einstein raises capital and has no skin in the game, he ultimately has nothing to lose, except your money.

Here is a little story about Einstein, and I don't mean Albert Einstein, the mathematical genius, but Einstein who is a modern self-proclaimed entrepreneur. He started many companies in his 35 years of life. His newest venture was inspired by going to his nephew's baseball game.

His sister and nephew were coming to the area that he lives in, because his nephew's travel team was playing in a baseball tournament.

He spent the weekend hanging out at the complex that hosted the tournament. He looked around at all the kids and their families who circulated through over the weekend in this huge multifield complex. Kids of all ages were playing ball. Little ones from 6 years old up to 18 years old filled this place from day to night. The vibe was energetic, positive, and lively.

He watched as each family pulled up in their big SUV with many different license plates from out of state. He started counting how many cars just paid for parking. He watched as thousands of people paid for the entrance fee over the course of the weekend. The snack stand had a line at all times. Parents lined up to sign their kids up to be videoed so they could have highlight reels accessible to market their kids for other programs, colleges, and major league baseball.

Cha-ching! Cha-ching!

And he got to thinking about how many parents invest in their kids playing sports. Then he continued to think about how much he loves baseball and how he enjoys being at his nephew's games. It is always a pleasant environment, well, almost always. Truth be told, you do get a crazy sore losing parent in there once in a while, but they add a little flavor to the game. Anyway, as his wheels started turning he really gave serious thought about how he could make a business out of this.

Einstein's Formula

Later on the week, he had an old friend from high school on the phone telling him about his new business adventure goal. He wanted to start a little league baseball brand of his own. He went on to tell his friend about how lucrative this investment could be. He couldn't believe how all of these parents spent thousands and thousands of dollars on their children to try make them baseball superstars or at least get them a college scholarship. Then there were the parents who wanted to give their kids the opportunity to have fun playing ball with their friends, and were willing to spend thousands on that.

He asked his buddy Joe if he'd be interested in investing. His buddy lives in a beach town and is a bartender and one of the local hot spots. As he went on pitching his idea to his longtime friend, he got more and more excited. Joe really liked the sound of the idea.

Joe and Einstein had met many years ago when Einstein was on a beach vacation and Joe was the bartender. They kept in touch through phone and text and would meet up to golf every few years.

His friend started getting excited along with him. But he didn't have any extra funds to throw in. However, he knew someone who did. There was a guy named Tyrone who often came to the bar. He came to mind because he was a serial investor. They would hang out a lot even when he wasn't at work. He was a big-time financial investor in the city and he was pretty flashy with his money. He was flashy in a way that he made everyone around him aware that he made a lot of money. He was definitely a big Mahoff. He told Einstein that he would talk to this guy about this opportunity.

Soon after, Joe introduced the two guys and they really hit it off. After a long phone conversation Einstein had Tyrone very excited! He pitched his idea and had his numbers all worked out. Everything sounded great! The numbers made sense. The return on investment was very appealing and Tyrone was very interested in investing in Einstein's little league tournament brand.

Soon after their chat, Tyrone called his cousin to tell him about his new investment opportunity. Cousin Charlie thought that sounded like a great opportunity! Charlie's son plays tournament ball and so he knows first-hand how much money parents spend on their kids for sports and just how lucrative this could be. Tyrone invited Charlie to participate in this business venture.

Tyrone comes back to Einstein ready to go! He even tells Einstein that he has another investor willing to match his capital contribution. Great for Einstein! So they both wire Einstein $15,000 each and off he goes to the baseball fields of Tennessee. In the meantime, the two cousins are up in Boston.

A few months later Charlie was out with his sister Georganne. They were catching up over a couple of beers and Charlie was telling her all about the little league team investment that he and Tyrone were doing. She started asking questions about their investment. Charlie didn't have many answers. It was Tyrone's project to monitor. Georganne was perplexed that Charlie wired some guy in Tennessee $15,000 months ago and has not heard one thing about the investment from either Tyrone or Einstein.

The next day Charlie called Tyrone. He didn't have any answers either. There had been no communication or updates up to this point. Georganne suggested that instead of calling Einstein for answers that they should head down there for a weekend trip to Tennessee. This way they could see exactly what their investment was paying for. Georganne accompanied her brother and her cousin.

They let Einstein know which weekend they were coming down. Einstein had a tour all planned out for them. He drove them from field to field showing them where all of the little league tournaments take place. But something didn't quite sit right with Georganne. She just had a strange feeling that something was off. She couldn't quite pinpoint it, but her gut was telling her to do some digging with this guy.

During the car ride she asked him some random questions about his personal life. His answers were vague. They stopped for lunch and when the check came Tyrone slid the bill over to Einstein. He told him that they gave him enough money and that he has to pay the lunch bill. Tyrone then stood up and said he would meet him in the car. Charlie stood up after him to follow him out. It was awkward to say the least. But Georganne stayed seated and continued sipping on her coffee. Tyrone looked back at Georganne and told her that it's time to go NOW. She told him that she would be out when she was finished with her coffee. Tyrone was obviously not happy that Georganne did not follow his lead and he then stormed out of the restaurant. Charlie follows Tyrone outside. Georganne and Einstein stayed seated at the table waiting for the server to come back to collect the check.

She looked at Einstein and laughed. She expressed to him how awkward that moment was. He was completely unphased by Tyrone's intentionally rude behavior. Einstein went on to tell Georganne that he's used to the big city folks coming down south acting like they're big shots (aka Mahoffs).

That statement peaked Georganne's interest. She asked him if he deals with city folks a lot. He went on to say that he did often. So Georganne continued to ask him some additional questions. She asked him what he did for a living before this business venture. He told her that he's always been an entrepreneur and he starts new businesses quite often, which is why he is used to dealing with the city boys from up north. She lined him up with questions, asking about his educational background and previous employers. She dug in and asked him if he was married or had kids. He said no to both. She asked him if he was in a relationship. He told her that he did but she didn't live around here. Georganne asked where she was living and he told her she lives in another country but she would be moving here to their country soon.

In the meantime, Tyrone and Charlie we're knocking on the window waving at them to hurry up. Georganne was ignoring them because she was actively, yet innocently, collecting information on the person who they invested in.

Before they got up to go outside, she nicely asked Einstein how many of his previous business that he was still involved in. Oblivious to Georganne's agenda, he let her know that none of the start-up companies that he previously started were still up and running. Georganne lightened up the conversation by sympathizing with him on the topic of running a business. In the meantime, her brain was about to explode because she knew how much money the guys gave to Einstein.

Then she asked the final question. She asked what average percentage of the financing he put in to start up any of the companies he was involved in previously. She also asked him if he took out small business loans from banks or does he stick with private investors. She had a feeling that she already knew the answer to these questions. He replied that he doesn't use his own money for his start-ups, he always finds outside investors. He also stated that he has never had to take a bank loan out because he easily finds people that will privately invest. He doesn't put skin in the game, so he ultimately has no risk. Georganne was trying to figure out if this guy was a serial dreamer or a flat out scammer. Needless to say, the little league baseball team idea ended just a few months later. The guys lost their money and Einstein disappeared.

I cannot stress this enough, as much as it is important to know what you're investing in, you must try your hardest to have a full understanding about who you're investing in. **Do your due diligence before giving anyone a cent.** Make sure you have a solid business plan as a point of reference before anything is in play.

Don't let anyone sell you a dream. Dreams do not happen without putting in the work first. There is always a risk involved in starting a business and in running a business, but just know that you're getting involved with someone who isn't going to hit it, then quit it. It comes down to protecting yourself and your money.

Questions

1. Would you invest in a business with someone that you don't know? Why? Why not?

   _____

   _____

   _____

2. What do you think Tyrone and Charlie could have done differently in this situation?

   _____

   _____

   _____

3. Why do you think Georganne wanted to stay with Einstein and drink her coffee when the other two guys left?

   _____

   _____

   _____

4. Do you believe in intuition and trusting your gut? Why? Why not?

   _____

   _____

   _____

Journal

What did you take from this chapter?

_____

_____

_____

_____

_____

CHAPTER 19

Choose Your Yuppy

Figure 19 Search for the best professional

Photo: Pekic/iStock by Getty Images

The word yuppy is often used in a negative light, if it is used at all. In the urban areas, middle class and lower income city folks look down on Yuppies. Personally, I never understood why it's used in a negative way.

By definition, yuppy stands for Young Urban Professional. A yuppy is typically a highly educated professional who has a good job, makes a nice living, and is overall successful. Lawyers, accountants, architects, insurance brokers, and so on; these are all examples of yuppies. A yuppy is typically a young adult who makes a lot of money in their profession. They like to spend that hard-earned money on a lavish lifestyle as well.

Maybe some people are intimidated by those who make more money or have a better education. It could be the fear of gentrification to their neighborhood. I don't know what it is. But it absolutely is a thing, hopefully that will change one day. People of a certain upbringing do not care for yuppies. I don't get it. They say things like "These Yuppies are ruining the neighborhood." Ummm, why are they ruining the neighborhood? Because they are buying up the abandoned dilapidated houses and fixing them up. This in turn improves the overall property value in an area. When property value improves, great things happen, and not-so-great things happen.

Now, at the risk of playing devil's advocate, let's get an understanding of the flip side. When property value goes up, the government usually takes advantage of the situation. Therefore, taxes increase and then people who have lived in these neighborhoods for years can't afford the tax increase. Landlords have to increase the rent to cover the cost of the tax increase and this is how people get pushed out of their neighborhoods and gentrification happens. But the reality of that is, it's not the yuppies' fault. That is the fault of the city or the town government that they live in. They do not have to increase the taxes of everyone just because some people can afford a higher tax. It should be priced accordingly to the newer buyers instead of penalizing those who have been loyal members of a community for their lifetime. A lot of cities provide tax abatements to people who buy brand new housing in lower income neighborhoods. The government lures people in with this tax break and they increase the taxes of everyone around them. Then when the tax abatement expires, the property is taxed hard. I find it to be completely unfair. So instead of being hostile toward the hardworking people who are fixing up the once-abandoned crack house on your street, take it up with the tax department. Not to mention that these yuppies spent a lot of money on their education. A lot of them have big loans to pay back and are working hard to do so.

Most people would love for their kids to grow up, get a good education and be a successful in whatever professional road they go down.

This leads me to a very important topic. Have you started to wonder about whom to choose to help you set up your business? We know that contractors are crucial to physically building out the space. We discussed how we need to check referrals and get at least three estimates for the scope of work needed. We touched on the importance of a financial planner. We also covered choosing your entity. How about the setting up of the actual business?

How are you going to choose the professionals who legally set up your business? Who's your yuppy? For starters, you are going to need an operating agreement and possibly a partnership agreement if necessary. The EIN is the employer identification number. It is used as the tax ID number for the business. Any company will need to obtain an EIN to set up their business, with the exception of a sole proprietorship. In that case you have the option to use your social security number instead of an EIN. These are the things you need to set up a basic business bank account. And we know that a business bank account is necessary to operate your biz.

You can set up your EIN directly through the Internal Revenue Service website or it can be set up through an accountant or attorney. You will need to know the type of entity that you will be setting up in advance. This is where hiring an experienced professional comes in handy. An attorney or an accountant who specializes in business will help you make the right decision as to what is the best type of entity that makes sense for you and your business.

Retain the Specialist

Cousin Estella is a lawyer. She has to know how to set up a business, so you think. Being that she is family, chances are that she isn't going to charge you much. Heck, she may even do it for free. Estella is part of a family law practice. She specializes in divorce and custody. She can handle these types of cases backward with her eyes closed.

Can she put together documentation to help set up your business? Sure she can. She is perfectly capable of putting together an operating agreement and a partnership agreement. But is she going to have the insight to forward think business wise and work in every important detail specific to your needs? Realistically speaking, she is probably not going to think of everything from a business standpoint. She just doesn't know how to. It's not what she does every day.

She can put together a basic legal document and fill in the blanks and that may work out to be fine. But it can also end in a business nightmare. There are many things that she just may not know how to work into the document.

This is where finding an experienced attorney who specializes in business is important. You may spend a little bit more than cousin Estella would charge you. But in the long run, it may save you thousands of dollars and lots of headaches by hiring someone who knows this type of practice like the back of their hand. They will help guide you and provide useful information so that you can develop smart and well thought-out business agreements.

The best way to find out about who to use is good old fashion word-of-mouth. Ask around to fellow business owners. Referrals from people who have had positive personal experiences go a long way. Shop local, right! Keeping it local is a smart decision if it is an option. People in a community want other people in their community to succeed.

If you don't know anyone who owns their own business you can seek out small business groups and ask there. You can head to your local community business association for referrals. There are lots of these groups found online, especially in social media platforms (Facebook and LinkedIn). Trusty old Google is a good alternative to take you to professional websites and sites to read reviews. This goes for all business professionals such as attorneys, accountants, and insurance agents.

Insurance is another expense to consider in your cost analysis. You will want to deal with an insurance agent who will help guide you to make sure you have the proper insurance for your business. Having a thorough understanding of your insurance needs can be very confusing, and with all of that fine print and legal mumbo jumbo you want to have someone that you trust present you with customized options that will suit your business needs.

If you rent space you may need renters insurance as well as business insurance. If you have rental insurance it's common for your landlord to state in the lease how much coverage is needed as well as make sure that you provide them with proof that they (the landlord) are listed as the additional insured.

You want to be informed about business liability and interruption insurance and what all of your options are. Your agent should help you determine the right amount of coverage necessary, based on your specific business needs.

Disability insurance is another type of insurance that you should look into. What happens if you are sick or injured and can't work? How are you paying your bills? Workers compensation insurance will help you with coverage if you get injured on the job. Workers comp is typically covered by your employer. This only applies if you are a W2 employee and not a 1099 employee.

What's the difference between being a W2 employee and a 1099 employee? A W2 is a tax document that is given to an employee who works for a specific company consistently. They are employees who are paid through payroll and taxes are taken out of their pay and paid to the government before they receive their pay. As the employer, you are responsible to record and withhold such taxes and make the city, state, and federal tax payments. The employer of a W2 employee is also responsible for contributing a percentage to each employee's tax requirements. A 1099 employee is basically an independent contractor. What that means is that you hire them to do work for your company. You directly pay them the pretaxed amount of payment and they are then responsible for handling their own taxes at the end of the year. You can use an accountant or a professional payroll processing company to handle tax with holdings. Companies such as ADP or Paychex are two of the named players in handling payroll. Or you can do it on your own with companies such as Turbo Tax or Taxfyle.

Regardless of which company you go with, you want to make sure that you use the right companies for these services because you don't want to mess around with your taxes and end up in a pickle. Make sure you do a review from time to time to make sure that they didn't make any mistakes. Tax jams are something we want to avoid at all costs! Not only can it leave us in a nightmare of a financial situation, but it can possibly lead to jail time in a federal prison. Keep in mind, these are all significant additional costs of doing business that you need to be prepared for.

As far as architecture, interior design, and space planning goes you can get experienced leads dealing with suppliers specific to your business. Using a retail store, for example, there are suppliers and distributors who sell wholesale products, supplies, and furnishings. In some cases, the distributors who sell furniture may have a space planner/interior designer on staff. In different businesses, there are different specs to follow according to the state regulations. In a hair salon, there has to be a specific amount of feet between each station. There also has to be a ratio of how many shampoo bowls to how many stations. And there is a maximum of stations according to the square feet of the space. This plays a part in plumbing and electric. Salons need dedicated electrical lines to each station to support the use of blow dryers and other tools that are used on the same outlet. You want someone who knows exactly what wattage is necessary and if you need to add additional electrical panels in order to support this. This is why it is important to work with a professional who is in tune with all of the codes and requirements, or you may not pass the inspection, and therefore will not be able to open your business.

The Work Environment

No matter what your business is, you want to work with someone who knows what they are doing specific to your business. It is imperative that you hire someone who is going to create a design that will utilize the space to use every square foot in a way that will generate maximum income.

Creating a workspace is more than just factoring esthetics. However, esthetics plays an important part to our businesses, our target market, and our employees. What kind of vibe do you want your business to have? It's safe to say that if you are about to open a sporting goods store, you're probably not going to go with a glittery pink theme and have the staff uniforms be ruffled tutu.

You want a design that is going to attract the right clients. Always remember that your vibe attracts your tribe.

Don't jump on the first recommendation. As always, get yourself two or three estimates so you have comparisons specifically related to both work details and cost. Read through the estimates carefully and make sure you understand exactly what services they state in writing that they will be providing. Don't assume that because you chatted about a specific something, that it is worked into the estimate. If it doesn't state it in the contract then it's most likely not going to happen. It may be a simple oversight, or they forgot to incorporate it altogether and will need to reevaluate the estimate.

At this point, if you do your homework you will have an understanding of how much you will be spending for the general start-up cost as well as business maintenance costs. Hopefully, this helps to prepare you for all the necessary expenses in starting up and keeping up your business afloat.

Once you have all of your prep work done it's time to let the fun begin! You dreamt about your business and now it is time to watch that dream turn into a reality. Get ready to work hard and grind until you can finally make a profit. Don't get discouraged because the fact is, it is going to take a while. Remember that you have to pay all of your investors, loans, and overhead expenses before you are able to pay yourself. But if you have grit and perseverance, you will get there!

Questions

1. What do you think about the word yuppy? Is it negative or positive and why?

   _____

   _____

   _____

2. If you plan to start your own business who would be the first person that you would talk to?

   _____

   _____

   _____

3. What do you need to get a business bank account set up?

   _____

   _____

   _____

4. Do you think that you have a better understanding of what it takes to start up and run a business? Why/Why not?

   _____

   _____

   _____

Journal

What did you take from this chapter?

_____

_____

_____

_____

_____

CHAPTER 20

Client Connections

Figure 20 Boosting loyalty to your firm

Photo: PixelsEffect/iStock by Getty Images

We are very fortunate to be able to run our businesses in this day and age of technology. It makes it very easy to connect with potential clients and current clients. Technology has invited businesses to send e-mails and texts and reach out to them through multiple social media platforms. Not to mention, the good old fashion postal service is always an option to connect with your clients. Any business owner should absolutely utilize all of these tools.

But what makes your company different? The information that you share with your clients about your company that boosts their loyalty to your firm, will encourage them to support your business. Let them get to know you. Share your background with them. Make sure that your client feels welcome and is sincerely appreciated.

Think about what makes a person want to patronize your business. There are many companies in your market that are just like yours out there, so why is yours so special? Let your customers and clients know what makes your company special. Allow that to be part of your brand.

Automated client e-mails and texts are super convenient for all businesses. But how many emails and texts is it going to take for your client to be annoyed by the fact that it is just too much. No one wants their e-mail accounts flooded, let alone with constant communication from the same company. So limit your communications to those messages that are important to solidifying your image. Find a welcomed balance.

Think outside the box. What are other ways that you can express to your clients just how much you appreciate each and every one of them. Sure, you can send them coupons or free samples, who doesn't like that? But you can also randomly call your client and thank them for their support. You can even mail them a handwritten note. It's very simple, and it lets people know that you appreciate them.

Personally speaking, I like to get to know my clients. I enjoy hearing people stories. Given my line of work, I am able to do so. I wholeheartedly appreciate connecting with my clients, and I hope that they realize just how much they are appreciated. I am also a natural-born helper. I want to help people and I want that to come through in my brand. I try to teach and mentor my employees to inspire all of our guests.

Avoiding Stress

How do you train someone in your employ to care like you care? Well for starters, I constantly remind my team that our guests have a huge selection of competitors to choose from and that we should appreciate that they chose us. I have also brought in a stress and anxiety coach to my salons to share with my team how to manage stress and share with our guests the same tactics. I promote wellness through group exercise team building classes and encourage our team to show the same encouragement to our clients.

I like to swap healthy recipes as well as delicious dessert recipes with clients as well. This is all part of building relationships. It is something that is important to me as a person and is a bonus as a business owner. I genuinely value these relationships. That is a hard thing to teach.

Now, there may be plenty of business owners that could care less about building relationships with their clients. Their clients are nothing but a number. That is their prerogative, if that's how they choose to deal with their clients. But I assure you that if you treat someone like they are just a number they will treat your business like it is just another company.

Loyalty as an Asset

If your business is viewed as just another company, do you think that adds value to your business? What about loyalty? Do you think if a client is treated like just another number that they will develop a sense of loyalty to your team and your business? These are just some things to give thought to. Expressing appreciation and gratitude goes so far.

Loyalty is priceless. Now, this is not to say that people can't support different businesses in the same industry; of course they can. If there is good rapport built between you and your clients, then they will know that they can always come back to you. And in a good business practice, you will welcome them with open arms. Never shame a client for going elsewhere; not only does it reflect poorly on your business but it is also makes them feel uncomfortable. Remember that a person may not remember what was said, they remember how you made them feel. That feeling applies in a positive way and in a negative one. Always try to keep your cool and keep clients feeling that they can always come back to you. This is if you want them to keep coming back.

A client that causes you/your company grief sometimes need to be broken up with. It doesn't have to be a nasty, screaming breakup. Sometimes it requires a simple conversation in which you express to them your issues with their behavior, and encourage them to give their business to someone else because you and your team can't seem to make them happy with your products or services. It's awkward; I am not going to indicate that it's not. But sometimes it needs to happen for the greater good of your business and your own sanity. But as a business owner, sometimes you have to have awkward conversations in order to get things straightened out. Who knows maybe they will take some time and return with a different attitude and have learned to even appreciate you and your business anew?

Questions

1. What are some ways for you to think of how you can express to your clients that you appreciate that they chose you and your business?

   _____

   _____

   _____

2. What are some ways for you to invite your clients to get to know you and get to know what your brand is about?

   _____

   _____

   _____

3. Would you want to build a relationship with your clients? Why or why not?

   _____

   _____

   _____

Journal

What did you take from this chapter?

_____

_____

_____

_____

_____

About the Author

Tara Acosta is a successful business owner in Philadelphia with two hair salons in two different sections of the city. She is also a stylist and barber of 20-plus years, giving her the opportunity to get to know many different people and hearing about a countless number of business successes and failures. Having multiple locations in the same industry provides a great comparison logistically.

In addition to her career as a successful salon owner, she has also overseen property rehabs and buildouts as well as participating in the project management of her and her husband's investment properties.

Tara and her husband together have financially invested in a broad range of business types. All of these business ventures have given Tara a depth of personal insight into the various scenarios played out behind the scenes in different commercial investments.

Her natural talent as a writer and businesswoman is combined in this, her first book, *The Street Smart Side of Business—A Behind-the-Scenes Guide to Making Smart Business Decisions.*

She has also written a novel, *North of Snyder.*

Tara resides in Philadelphia with her husband and three children: Cianna, Anthony, and Jaxon.

Index

OTHER TITLES IN THE BUSINESS CAREER DEVELOPMENT COLLECTION

Vilma Barr, Consultant, Editor

- *Fast Forward Your Career* by Simonetta Lureti and Lucio Furlani
- *Ask the Right Questions; Get the Right Job* by Edward Barr
- *100 Skills of the Successful Sales Professional* by Alex Dripchak
- *Negotiate Your Way to Success* by Kasia Jagodzinska
- *Personal and Career Development* by Claudio A. Rivera and Elza Priede
- *Getting It Right When It Matters Most* by Tony Gambill and Scott Carbonara
- *How to Make Good Business Decisions* by J.C. Baker
- *The Power of Belonging* by Sunita Sehmi
- *Your GPS to Employment Success* by Beverly A. Williams
- *Emotional Intelligence at Work* by Richard M. Contino and Penelope J. Holt
- *The Champion Edge* by Alan R. Zimmerman
- *Shaping Your Future* by Rita Rocker-Craft
- *Finding Your Career Niche* by Anne S. Klein

Concise and Applied Business Books

The Collection listed above is one of 30 business subject collections that Business Expert Press has grown to make BEP a premiere publisher of print and digital books. Our concise and applied books are for...

- Professionals and Practitioners
- Faculty who adopt our books for courses
- Librarians who know that BEP's Digital Libraries are a unique way to offer students ebooks to download, not restricted with any digital rights management
- Executive Training Course Leaders
- Business Seminar Organizers

Business Expert Press books are for anyone who needs to dig deeper on business ideas, goals, and solutions to everyday problems. Whether one print book, one ebook, or buying a digital library of 110 ebooks, we remain the affordable and smart way to be business smart. For more information, please visit www.businessexpertpress.com, or contact sales@businessexpertpress.com.

CPSIA information can be obtained
at www.ICGtesting.com
Printed in the USA
BVHW051637010522
635780BV00007B/221